College Tuition:

Four Decades of
Financial Deception

Robert V. Iosue • Frank Mussano

Blue River Press
Indianapolis, Indiana

College Tuition: Four Decades of Financial Deception
©2014 by Dr. Robert V. Iosue & Dr. Frank Mussano

Published by Blue River Press
2402 N. Shadeland Avenue, Suite A
Indianapolis, Indiana 46219
www.brpressbooks.com
A Tom Doherty Company, Inc. imprint

Distributed by Cardinal Publishers Group
317-352-8200 phone
317-352-8202 fax
www.cardinalpub.com

ISBN: 978-1-935628-39-2

Cover Design: Phil Velikan
Proofread by: Charleen Davis
Book design by: Dave Reed

Printed in the United States of America

10 9 8 7 6 5 4 3 2 1

Contents

Charts

Acknowledgements

The authors would like to thank Carol Innerst for her welcome review of the manuscript.

Separately, Author Robert V. Iosue would like to thank all the people he worked with at C.W. Post College for 16 years as professor, dean and vice president, with special focus on former presidents Ed Cook and now deceased former president Bob Payton, both of whom led the institution with strength and class. Special thanks to mathematics mentor Professor Herb Kranzer, respected professor of mathematics at Adelphi University, who patiently guided me through my PhD. Special thanks to all at York College of Pennsylvania where, as president, I was able to try out various ideas that incorporated cost containment. With their help, we all succeeded in making it a better institution. Finally I would like to thank my family for their forbearance with my all-consuming fixation on cost containment. As my son said, "Is it worse growing up in the great depression, or in having a father who did?"

Author Frank Mussano extends a warm thank you to his family, especially his wife Pat, for her support and understanding as he pounded away at the computer keys night after night into the wee hours of the morning. I am deeply grateful to Kathy Shaub for lending her expertise to format and proofread the early stages of the manuscript - without her skillful guidance I could have never figured out all of those crazy, nonintuitive formatting nuances. To my friends at York College of Pennsylvania, an institution that has served as a model of efficiency, thank you for the incredible ride which inspired much of the material in this book. Finally, I must express my utmost gratitude to our publisher, Tom Doherty, and his amazing team. Tom is the consummate professional who skillfully and patiently shepherded this project to fruition with his competent leadership while involving us in the process every step of the way. It has been our good fortune to work with the best!

Preface

So, why read this particular book about the cost of higher education? After all, there are probably thousands of writings on the subject. Well, the difference here is that the authors are seasoned, knowledgeable insiders who have been exposed to the frustrating, illusionary techniques of college tuition hocus pocus over multiple decades. We are finally pulling away the curtains to reveal the smoke and mirrors that have been steadfastly – and successfully – used to justify outrageous price increases year after year.

Our goals are simple. We're hoping to motivate parents and students who are struggling with the daunting process of choosing a college to enact change by voicing their informed concerns, and ultimately selecting a focused, well-run institution. This book will help college-bound students use free online search engines and college databases to identify cost-effective schools while taking advantage of techniques to secure the most beneficial financial aid opportunities.

Furthermore, the general public, the media, and college contributors should be so concerned about the tactics and laissez-faire attitudes we describe and document, that there will be a strong effort to spur policymakers, board members, presidents, and employees at every college and university to speak more forcefully, and with more ammunition and authority, on the subject of institutional finances. It is time for a strong effort to reel in the unconscionable inefficiencies that have enveloped our formerly esteemed higher education system. These attitudes have allowed one of the longest ongoing deceptions to continue in America.

Finally, we ask that colleges and universities be challenged to formally and accurately audit and justify their work productivity and subsequent fee structures at all levels. This should include both faculty and non-teaching staff. Ultimately, isn't that what the best organizations do to ensure that they are providing the utmost value for their customers? As our well-documented and easily-read data indicates, we have no doubt whatsoever that the significant dollars diverted to outlandish, wasteful expenditures and inefficiencies can and should be reverted back to families and their children, the future payers and consumers of college education.

The title of this brief book makes clear that costs: tuition, room and board, and a bewildering assortment of fees are the main subject. *College Tuition: Four Decades of Financial Deception* does not go into the classroom. We do not attack or question teaching proficiency, nor do we challenge the class material or subjects in which students major. There are books in which the authors stress the traditional programs and courses of study. We do not quarrel with them. But we are compelled to point out that changes have occurred in our country, and we must acknowledge, and respond positively to some of them. Consider our history of higher education beginning in the mid 1600s; only available for males. They would have three academic outcomes from which to choose a major: a doctor, a theologian, or a gentleman. Small but steady changes followed, but in the mid to latter 1800s, the change brought about by the Morrill Act was monumental. It resulted in basic sciences, agriculture, and even mechanical arts joining the liberal arts at many of our colleges. In the early 1900s teacher training went from two and three-year programs to complete acceptability within the four-year curriculum. And the formerly three-year hospital-based nursing program became a four-year staple at many of our colleges. There were, and still are, many changes going on, some prompted internally, and many more encouraged by outside forces. It reminds us of what Di Lampedusa said (paraphrasing) in *The Leopard*, "If you want things to stay the same, then we will have to make some changes."

Because of the ever-changing world outside of the Ivory Tower, we in higher education must also continue to change. College graduates with a well-balanced education – a major that will get them a good job, along with a core of traditional solid academic courses that will enrich and ennoble them mentally – is not a disagreeable change. In other words, while liberal arts programs and courses must remain on just about all of our four-year colleges and universities, we must add to these permanent, valuable fixtures many new and varied studies that will equip graduates to find vocations in the big, fast-moving world. Some colleges market their new career-oriented programs openly; some do it in more quiet ways; some do not broadcast their additions; and a small handful have not made many changes at all. The variety and multiple choices for incoming students is one of the blessings of our diverse system. We are in a position to accommodate and educate virtually any student with almost any goal.

Unfortunately, the cost to attend the vast majority of our colleges and universities, public as well as private, has changed precipitously over the last four decades. The cost of attending is a wall of monumental height.

In 1987, the previous 10 years of tuition increases seemed unbearable, and laments were heard across the country. The media was on the back of every college that raised its tuition at a rate of twice the cost of living. The government vowed to bring the increases to a halt. The people were incensed. Something had to be done; it could not continue. Congress, in 1987, formed a special committee to look into the matter, with members chosen by the Senate, the House, and the president. I served on the committee for three years, while continuing to write about the waste in higher education. The year 1990 came and went, along with more than a score of additional years of on-again, off-again complaints. But nothing changed. From 1973-74 to the present, tuition and fees have risen on average more than twice the cost of living. Neither the media nor the government could slow down the financial onslaught.

It was at this time, in 1987, that the director of the University of Illinois Press called and asked if I would write a book about the causes of the ever-increasing costs of higher education. My first response was that I did not have the time. He prevailed by promising to assign an editor who would assist if I sent a rough draft, and suggested that a compilation of my past articles accompanied with testimony given before congressional committees would be a good beginning.

For a university press to even consider a book stressing the financial waste on campuses across America would be an act of bravery. The rough draft was submitted and acknowledged, but beyond that, never moved forward. It sat for close to 25 years while tuition levels continued their inexorable upward surge, leaving financial ruin and serious ethical questions in their wake. One might speculate how any endeavor of any kind could continue for so long to extract exorbitant rates from the public. This was because there were relatively few economic setbacks during the 1980s, 1990s, and into the 2000s. Nor were there any real periods of high unemployment. Best of all, recent college graduates did not have much trouble finding jobs. Also, graduates may have had some debt to take care of, but it was manageable. None of this is true now – yet the increases still exceed twice the cost of living.

In 2014, after some 40 years of twice-the-cost-of-living increases, this book has become the road map of higher education's duplicity and deception in most matters dealing with finances. The light of day has to be shined on the reasons why a once dignified endeavor has become one of the most self-serving institutions in America.

I asked my colleague of many years, Dr. Frank Mussano, to add to this chilling piece of history delineated in the first section of the book, additional reasons why higher education has to reform itself. He has added demographics, tuition discounting, technology, government-backed loans, and other concerns, as well as a series of compelling easy-to-decipher charts indicating that the cost of going to college has been exacerbated by recent trends and continues to be the major problem that needs attention, if this listing ship is to survive. He also lent his expertise in college search services and financial aid award procedures to offer practical, cost-saving approaches for college-bound students and their parents as they navigate through the bewildering college selection process.

The first section of this book briefly describes the genesis of the accelerated tuition trajectory that began in the early 1970s. There are few charts, and the statistics are limited both in depth and in number. But the message is abundantly clear. It plainly describes how colleges and universities across the country had begun a march toward financial profligacy that has continued unabatedly to the present era.

The second section provides more detail and confirmation that self-centered designs and actions have moved the vast majority of institutions of higher education away from service to society and directed them toward self-interest and financial self-regard.

Students are the Crabgrass on My Academic Lawn!

We do not know who first said it, but this has become the quiet mantra of professors across the country, aided by bloated fleets of administrators and our overly-generous government.

Over the years, we have been asked one question more than any other. "Why does college cost so much?" Of course, the person asking (and without exaggeration, there have been, and continue to be, thousands asking that question) wanted a direct uncomplicated answer. This book provides that answer along with equally direct and uncomplicated solutions. Mark Twain's answer to complicated questions was to the effect that there were always two sides, or, as he picturesquely said it, 'I never saw a one-sided pancake.' The reader of this book will soon see that there are direct, uncomplicated answers; that there are not two sides to every question. They will also see that too many college administrators and professors try their best to obfuscate both the reasons for the perpetual high increases along with any possible resolutions.

The book concludes with solutions that will help colleges save themselves. It also provides practical guidance to college-bound students and their parents for using the wealth of available free resources to find colleges that offer the best bang for the buck, and for implementing proven techniques to land the best financial aid deal.

Dr. Robert V. Iosue

General Comment

Individually, the authors sometimes talk about their personal experiences in the first person, without identifying themselves. This style works well because the two collaborators speak with one voice and perspective throughout the book, resulting in a seamless and more coherent narrative for the reader.

College Tuition:

Four Decades of Financial Deception

The History of Colleges' Disregard for Exorbitant Costs

The way college costs are skyrocketing at most colleges is tragic. Our middle class family is considering not sending our three kids to college, even though they test in the 99th percentile on school achievement tests and my husband and I both graduated from college. We would feel more inclined to sacrifice our retirement savings for their education if there was less waste of our money.

This letter came from the heartland of America's Midwest. It could have come from any place in the United States. It was a plea directed to the overwhelming majority of our colleges and universities, and it is not an isolated appeal for relief. It was a universal plea to stop the unnecessary and exorbitant tuition increases that were relentless. What is shocking is that the letter was written in 1987, and came after over 10 years of incessant tuition increases. Those increases, measured at twice the rate of the national Consumer Price Index (CPI) started in the mid 1970s and have been virtually automatic since then.

Before we get into details confirming why the exorbitant tuition increases are unwarranted, let me offer an unverified explanation as how it initially started. We will use the fashionable technique of blaming one or more of the Ivy League colleges for any fault whose initiator is suspect. The eight Ivy League colleges certainly knew they had name appeal. And for reasons well-understood, what one or more of the Ivies do, other colleges will follow. Being called one of the top schools in the country not only lends prestige, but allows it to add a little to the tuition. Some people are willing to pay extra for name value. The year 1973 comes as close as can be expected for the beginning of tuition increases that capitalized on supply and demand, accompanied by pure name value.

One might think of it as a "premium" paid for name attachment. This in no way demeans the high quality of these colleges. Rather, without making internal changes, while at the same time exploiting the name, one could charge more. It was dubbed The Chivas Regal Effect, indicating that the label could be as important as the contents. The other Ivy League schools, being in strong competition for similarly intellectually endowed students, followed suit. The Ivy League schools mounted a rising assault on tuition, so dramatically in accord with each other, and for more than 15 years, that the federal Justice Department accused them of being a cartel, after adding MIT into the mix. It was still an era when just about all colleges tried to emulate the elites, so tuition, room, and board started to increase at colleges across the country, continuing at an average rate of twice the cost of living from 1975 to the present. This is a faster rate of increase over a longer period of time, than any other commodity, business, service, or endeavor – including medical costs.

One statistic alone will illustrate the vast sweep the tuition rise took over a 60-year period when compared with household income and with the overwhelming increases taking place between 1975 and the present. In 1947 the national average household income was $3,031, and the cost to attend Harvard was $455; an amount equal to approximately 15 percent of the family income. By 2011 the average family income was $50,054, while Harvard's tuition and fees (not room, board, or assorted other fees) jumped to $36,305; which turns out to be 73 percent of the family salary. By 2014, tuition and fees had expanded to $43,938 while family income remained relatively stagnant at about $50,000; which comes to almost 88%. Room and board, along with other expected costs puts the total well above $60,000 a year. As expected, a vast number of other colleges followed their lead.

There are approximately 3,600 institutions of higher education in the country, not counting the many for-profits that have sprung up across the country with much vigor. Indeed, there are so many of them professing to cater to the needy student and consuming so much of the federal student aid budget that concerns have been expressed about some of their goals. Does the profit motive trump the education of the student, as some claim? Or is it the other way around?

Not quite half of the traditional non-profit institutions are public, yet about 75 percent of students attend these public institutions, and 25 percent attend private institutions. The cost has become alarmingly high at far too many of them – whether private or public. How do our colleges respond to the unwarranted increases? Unfortunately, one of the best played games in higher education is to treat every criticism with disdain: "Anecdotes, just anecdotes" or "The criticizer doesn't understand the special nature of our particular college" or "The criticism doesn't apply to my particular college," or a statement that next year will be better. The problem, simply stated, is that we have not remained faithful stewards of our colleges' finances. Our cost-containment efforts are weak or nonexistent. We would rather pay more money and attention to increases in enrollment than to controlling the budget.

Since 1988 there has been a valid concern over the high cost of running our institutions of higher education. Emblematic of the concern during the late 1980s was a cartoon in a West Coast newspaper that shows a mother with tears in her eyes, as she watches her son drive off to college with the car sagging under the weight of boxes, saying: "It's so sad to see him headed off to college with his luggage full of his belongings." The father, with a surprised look, exclaims: "Belongings? That's this semester's tuition!" In a survey of students done at this time, under the aegis of the Council for Advancement and Support of Education, fully 48 percent of those surveyed said they thought the major reason more students did not go to college was because it was too expensive and they could not afford it.

It was during this period that I published an article in a national newspaper titled "How Colleges Can Cut Costs". The reaction was much more substantial than expected. I had published articles on the same subject, the first one going back to 1975 titled, "Who Pays for the High Cost of Low Tuition", an article dealing primarily with the high hidden costs of public institutions accompanied by the low workload of professors who teach there. The reaction was lukewarm and soon forgotten, as was the reaction to other articles written on the subject of high costs.

But the latest article essentially blamed colleges and universities for the unusually high costs and pointed out where waste in higher education occurred, mainly consisting of increased bureaucracy and reduced professorial teaching loads; the reaction was extensive. Indeed, the media picked up on the issue, and the Department of Education renewed its efforts to control costs. Yet the problem of excessively increasing costs continued unabatedly.

While we in higher education profess it to be a place of tolerance of ideas and a protector of freedom of speech, we do not take kindly to nor tolerate criticism. We have long enjoyed an insular existence, a somewhat exalted position, and like the church of old, have come to believe we are deserving of a sacrosanct position in society. But a change was occurring. The dean of a large university thought so highly of the article he had it printed verbatim in his college's alumni journal and sent it to more than 34,000 alumni. He added his own words of caution about waste and low productivity, and it pleased me greatly to know that finally there was an ally. Unfortunately, he closed his comments with a notice of his retirement from academe.

The executive director of a small company recited his history in his letter. He was a tenured associate professor just about to be promoted to full professor at a state university of some renown; he had written two books and numerous articles, taught one graduate-level course and three undergraduate level courses, served on many committees, and had time left over for research. He also operated a business on the side. He loved it all and had attained the not-so-ripe old age of 35. Why did he leave this ideal situation? He left because he could no longer tolerate a group of professors, some of them with senior rank, who did no more than a total of 20 hours' worth of work a week. As he put it:

> **I just got worn out by being surrounded by vociferous mediocrity.**

This sentiment reminds us of a three-part series written by Richard Louv, an award-winning reporter for the *San Diego Union-Tribune*, a series he aptly titled "Eduflation." He begins one part of the series with the description of a relatively highly paid professor (which from experience and knowing the area and the institution I would put in the $60,000 or so bracket (remember, it's 1986; by 2012, a full professor's salary would be more than $150,000) who had decided "kickback time had come." The professor had been extraordinarily dedicated to the students he taught, but now had moved to an expensive condo on the beach and was teaching only one course per semester.

If we jump to the present, almost three decades later, both authors were discussing progress on this book at a local restaurant when a professor we knew came over to chat with us. Obviously, he did not know what we were doing. He proceeded to tell us what a wonderful sinecure he had, how much the many breaks in the semester afforded him time to travel, how short the semesters really were, and the kicker was his statement that "he had paid his dues and now kickback time had arrived." We were stunned for three reasons: he was not that old, he was never overworked, and his words were the words, almost verbatim, of so many others.

Research was not the reason for such a low teaching load; having "paid one's dues" was. Now it was time to live off the system like so many others. Mr. Louv goes on to report that higher education has anointed itself to be a High Church, a sacred trust that is running at twice the rate of inflation. His book has captured the ill will and resentment that is gradually and surely being directed at this "sacred trust" – a trust, I might add, that has lost its way.

A businessman wrote to say how much he deplored the waste, and went on to say that for years he employed the chairmen of departments at two major universities on a consulting basis. He used them a lot and asked them how they could be away from their teaching jobs for so much time. "No problem" was the answer. The community relations person of one of the world's largest chemical companies wrote that he teaches a course on the graduate level in addition to working at his full-time job. He called faculty lazy and said they publish mostly for each other. Obviously he is generalizing, but his perceptions do reflect the growing views of an awfully large segment of the population. From the dean of a community college in the Northwest comes a real beaut:

> **Add my name to the list of colleagues who support your position on reckless spending. Colleges and universities are the 'black hole' of state budgets. We suck in every dollar that comes within gravitational reach of our hungry mouths without even addressing issues of prioritization of needs or internal relocation of funds out of tired and marginal programs.**

An Ohio professor wrote that over the 30 years he was a college teacher, he has seen too much bureaucratic growth in public institutions and too little teaching by many of his colleagues. He also observed that dissension on these matters was discouraged.

That there is a problem, starting in the mid 1970s and continuing well into the 21st century, cannot be denied. The problem is real and will not go away on its own, nor can it be talked away by those responsible for the inordinate increases. It is fair to say that the media has clung to this issue for a longer period of time than any other single matter, in part because it is newsworthy, and mostly because the higher education community has given no rational justification for the excessive tuition increases.

And this lack of a logical or sincere reassurance from the higher education community has produced the longest, most extensive, and most unsympathetic media reaction than has occurred against such high profile systems such as medical care or, everyone's favorite, the Department of Defense. Just a few of the hundreds of article headlines from the 1980s should convince the public that not much has changed as colleges continue their flight to the top of the tuition crest.

> "Ahead: Another Big Jump in College Tuition,"
> *U.S. News & World Report*, April 8, 1985.
>
> "Are We Spending Too Much on Education?"
> *Forbes*, December 29, 1986.
>
> "Education: Facing Up to Sticker Shock," *Time*,
> April 20, 1987.
>
> "Our Greedy Colleges," *The New York Times*,
> February 18, 1987.
>
> "Fuming Over College Costs," *Newsweek*, May
> 18, 1987.
>
> "Students in the Hole: How Much Debt is Too
> Much?" Summer, 1987.

What ought to be impressive about the above selection of headlines is not their cleverness, but their common theme. Each of the articles appeared in national or large regional newspapers or magazines, and they represent only a few of the ones that appeared. Equally impressive are the dates represented; and yet, more than 25 years later, nothing has changed. Both private and public schools have raised their total fees for almost four decades without regard for people's ability to pay. (It's worth noting that another 1988 headline, not included in the above list, hauntingly raises the following question: "The Class of 2010: How Will They Pay?" Spring, 1988. Nostradamus could not have made a better prediction).

There obviously were thousands more that dwelled on the same themes. The concern over high college costs today did not just emerge, it is a concern of long duration and it remains of abiding interest. We in higher education have tried our hardest to obfuscate the issue and be less than accurate in explaining the high costs. Smoke and mirrors is not too severe an indictment.

In June 1988, a Special Advisory for College and University Presidents was issued by a National Task Force on Higher Education and the Public Interest: Of the five public interest questions, the price and cost of higher education is of greatest concern to the public and educators alike:

> **Fewer still understand the relationship of price to cost in either public or independent colleges and universities, or the pricing differences between the sectors. The price/cost question also has become closely tied to an urgent national problem. When the principal economic challenge for the nation is whether American goods and services can be made and marketed as cheaply and as well as those of other nations, it should not be surprising that concerns about productivity have spread to higher education.**

> **How colleges and universities respond to the price/cost issue will influence long-term regulatory responses by federal and state governments. The imposition of governmental controls on the health care industry is particularly instructive, and a similar fate may await higher education. Such controls could affect public and private institutions alike.**

The public doesn't necessarily want more information on the reasons behind tuition increases. Parents and students, especially, want reassurances that college will be affordable. Not being able to attend college is an unacceptable alternative.

While we applaud their accuracy and their candor, even their courage to use the dreaded word "productivity" when we talk of education, we have to wonder why their advisory came so late in the game. More importantly, why has nothing changed over the last few decades since this and other similar reports have come out? We also have to wonder why college presidents and their boards of trustees keep raising costs at alarming rates, and higher education lobbyists keep asking for more and more government money, unmindful of impending government controls. As the advisory warns us, if we follow the path set by health care, won't government control closely follow? What is there about higher education that allows itself to believe that it is above even the most elementary levels of financial accountability? What allows it to ask for more and more money from our students; demand more of our local, state and federal taxes; and still retain the fiction of societal service and independence?

Being held in high esteem can carry us only so far. In 1985, the National Association of Independent Colleges and Universities sought to discover the perception held by the public toward private colleges. The report titled "Parents' Views About Independent Colleges and Universities" concluded that the public believes that private colleges are "prohibitively expensive." Today, everyone knows that colleges are "prohibitively expensive." But, it was new and startling news in 1985.

Let us look at a few statistics that will convince even the most sympathetic of people that colleges' handling of finances is running amok. During the period of 1980–86, there had been an average annual increase in college tuition of 10.6 percent. This yearly increase was more than double the yearly increase in the cost of all goods and services, which was 4.8 percent. Even more compelling was the fact that college increases were about 25 percent higher than those of medical care over the same period. During a period when medical care costs had risen dramatically and we had subjected the medical field to blistering attacks, higher education outperformed them with 10.6

percent per year increases, as compared to medical care's 8.5 percent raises.

During the same period, the price of houses rose an average of 6.1 percent, food rose an average of 3.9 percent, new cars rose an average of 3.8 percent, and energy was fairly flat. It would be difficult to find a commodity or a service that rose faster and went further than higher education costs. Actually, the problem goes further back than most people realize, including those who claim the dramatic tuition increases are recent and serve to make up lost time. Between 1970 and 1986, the consumer price index rose 182 percent while college tuition soared by 232 percent, a total of 50 percentage points higher.

The high cost of college is not a recent phenomenon; it has just become more noticeable, more outlandish, and those defending it more arrogant and at times just plain silly in their defense. If nothing is done to hold down the increases over a sustained period, future costs will become more absurd and jeopardize our entire system of higher education, along with its intended purpose of providing opportunity for all who can benefit from it. This begs the question, discussed in Chapter 7, about whether we are reaching the point where many families believe that a college education simply isn't worth the outrageous investment.

Let us take as an example a private college charging $14,000 for room, board, tuition, and other fees, which was the 1989 average. Using an average 8 percent increase as a guide, one can expect to pay $48,000 for the same one-year package in 16 years at our average private college. Later in the book, you will see numbers that are higher than that. When private institutions jumped 9 percent on average for the 1988–89 year and the Consumer Price Index (CPI) rose only 4 percent, many college administrators and educational lobbyists said that we should not compare apples to oranges; we should not compare the increases in higher education to the increases in consumer prices because their makeup is different. Of course they are different, just as surely as it's different for any other activity, be it a church, the medical profession, the defense industry, the automobile industry, or shoe repairs.

Any particular business or endeavor could claim immunity from the consumer price index on the basis of apples to oranges. But it's the best we have, and since everyone else is subject to its measure – including Social Security increases and rising costs in the medical field, (which could easily claim that practicing defensive medicine should relieve it of the criticism received because of large increases) – then why should the higher education establishment be immune from comparisons with the consumer price index? An even more compelling reason to accept the CPI as a fair measuring device is that families throughout the country often receive increases based mainly on it.

We in education have our national lobbying organizations located in Washington fighting tooth and nail for every cent and every break we can get from our government just like any other lobbyist representing any other self-interested commercial enterprise. Some put higher education's lobby seventh from the largest, peddling their influence. They conduct their business from One Dupont Circle, and care little for which federal aid program they insist must be heavily funded. If asked to set a priority, their answer would be: "All of the above!" Our larger educational institutions, public and private, have their own full-time lobbyists at the state and federal levels trying to influence the lawmakers in exactly the same way the automobile industry, the defense industry, or the farming industry does it. Whether it's favorable legislation or more tax subsidies, or product protection, the similarity of actions is very apparent. Yet there are those who want to hold all others accountable for outlandish price increases *except* higher education, usually on the basis that "it's different." Or we use the disingenuous argument offered by the president of one of our national higher educational organizations:

> **Students and their families should not be discouraged by these increases; proper family financial planning and financial aid can put higher education within the reach of almost any qualified student.**

Somehow I don't think our Midwestern family with three bright kids will easily swallow that line. At $48,000 per kid, that comes to a cool $144,000 per year they'd better be ready to shell out when all three are in college.

Not only is it a serious problem, it is one that has remained with us. In 1988, in one of my articles it was stated that if left alone, prices would rise at the same unconscionable rates they had for the previous decade, i.e., at twice the CPI rate. For the 1987–88 year, the increase for private colleges was 8 percent, while the consumer price index was a meager 3.7 percent. There was a justifiable public outcry at the time. The American Council on Education did a survey and found that college administrators predicted that increases for the next year, 1988–89, would slow down to about 4 or 5 percent, thereby soothing the public outcry and placating irate parents, students, and politicians. The college year 1988–89 arrived, and with it came an average 9 percent increase for private colleges. Nor could the consumer price index be blamed, since it rose a little less than four points. If the record is any indication, the majority of our college administrators are not the ones to solve this problem. They most certainly are the problem.

Regrettably, they are the principal source of the lamentable position we are now in, and their predictions of reduced tuition increases are used as a balm to get the media and the public off their backs. When we predicted a 4 percent to 5 percent increase for 1988–89, and then came in at an average 9 percent, our credibility was unsalvageable. There was not an energy crisis to blame for our extraordinary increase; there was no shortage of students to blame. So we traipsed out the same old, tired, unimaginative clichés we've used year-after-year. More will be said later about academia's response to all these increases, but one response deserves attention now because it is the type of response that is so deft that it tricks both the media and the public into sometimes believing these increases are entirely justified.

A fine small (2,000 students) private institution announced its fees would increase about 10 percent, an increase that caused its fees to go from $6,410 eight years previous to $15,260 for the 1988–89 year. By way of explanation, the college announced that its full-time assistant professors had dramatic salary increases of $12,100 over the same period, going from $17,500 to $29,600 over eight years. The college left it for others to figure out that the fees increased by 138 percent while the salaries increased by only 69 percent. Nor did they inform the public that all faculty would no longer be expected to teach three courses in one semester and four in the second semester. They would teach only three each semester. Anyone with even an elementary interest in pricing strategies could determine that they had to charge an outrageous tuition to cover a 14 percent decline in teaching productivity accompanied by large increases in compensation.

The media are very capable of reporting the information they are fed, but often are not as skilled as they should be when it comes to asking the right questions or ferreting out the details. And duplicity grows on campuses as transparency disappears, making it even tougher for reporters to get the truth. Of course, we in higher education do know how to hide things, and we still enjoy a modicum of trust.

Public colleges are no better than are private colleges when it comes to financial stewardship. During the period from 1980–81 to 1986–87, the average annual increase in tuition at public colleges was 9.8 percent, while the average annual increase in the Consumer Price Index was 4.9 percent during the same period. Tuition for public colleges is only part of the cost, and a relatively small part at that. On average, about 20 percent used to come from tuition, and the rest from taxes at the local, state, and federal level, plus fund-raising, which was the exclusive province of private institutions, but has now become de rigueur at all public institutions. Public institutions enjoy a cost advantage over private institutions because even a large increase of 9.8 percent on a low tuition does not amount to a large amount of money. Students who attend public universities today pay more than 20% of the full tuition, but much of that is from loans, as you shall see in the section dealing with the impending loan crisis.

During the early 1980s the average public institution might raise its $1,600 tuition bill by 9.8 percent, which comes to an increase of $157, hardly an unbearable increase. At the same time, a private institution might raise its $9,000 tuition by 9.8 percent, which is a sizable $882 increase. Room, board, and fees would be additional and go up accordingly. Public colleges and universities enjoy an enviable position in another way when it comes to jacking the price up. If they do not get all the tax dollars they ask, they use the time-honored device of quickly pointing out to the legislators (and the newspapers) that they must then raise tuition some astronomical amount, thereby putting the students and parents on notice that the bad guys are in political office, and that perhaps they ought to pressure them for more tax dollars so they can hold tuition increases to a reasonable level.

It's a game played out each year, with the result generally being that tax dollars are increased at a larger rate than the CPI, and tuition receives its usual extra-large increase. The end result is a very expensive public system replete with underworked faculty and overstaffed administrations. Over the years there has been a gradual, but definite shift in enrollment from private to public, in part because the quality of public institutions now rivals that of the private colleges, and in large part because of the lower tuition. Historically, public institutions were designed to accommodate the middle and lower income families, while the private colleges had a more elite atmosphere about them and educated many more higher-income students. Much of this has changed over the years, whereby even families with very large incomes send their kids to well-regarded public universities. And many private schools, especially those that lost their elite appeal, or never attained it, attract many middle and lower income kids, along with first family members to attend college.

Some research has been done, usually on a state level, to attempt to determine whether the public higher education system is more or less expensive than private colleges. A study conducted by the U.S. Department of Education showed that, on average, a public institution was slightly less costly than a private one. The flaw with the study was that it did not include all the hidden costs associated with public institutions, costs that cannot be hidden by private institutions. For example, the costs of central administrations of public institutions are not allocated to any particular public college. As a matter of fact, there are so many hidden costs, or costs that are not accounted for, in public institutions that it is very difficult to get an accurate comparison. Difficult, but not impossible.

In 1974, an intensive study was conducted to find the true cost of the State University of New York, known as the SUNY system, and to make comparisons with private institutions. The study, published in 1975, compared apples to apples, which was no easy task. For example, if a private college has a mortgage on a classroom building or floated a bond to build a dormitory, the interest payments, which can be considerable, are part of the college budget in just the same way a mortgage payment on a home is part of a family expense. Not so for the public colleges, because the central state offices floated the bonds, or tax monies were provided to build the building, so no payments are made from the public college budget.

At one private college I worked at, the mortgage payments were fully 10 percent of the entire college budget, and of course the 10 percent is passed along to the students in higher tuition and fees. For the public institution, no such expense occurred, since taxes covered the cost of the bonds, and were not found in the college budget. The study showed that a costly traveling bookmobile that serviced the public institutions was not expensed to any single college, but rather to a central budget that each individual college could ignore when figuring the total cost of running its campus. We found that heating oil was billed centrally; and, therefore, was not assigned to any particular public college. These and other costs were not included in the cost of running a public college, but every private college has to include every such expense. When each and every expense was included for public college, it easily reached the average cost of running a private college.

What we found was that our public colleges and universities are just as expensive as our private ones, and in some cases more expensive. We also found that the teaching load for faculty at one of the larger public institutions was an average 1.45 courses per semester. One need not be an economics major to conclude that with that scant teaching load, the cost of running the place was going to be outrageously high.

Public institutions are in general no different in total cost than are private institutions. Their tuition is considerably lower because of tax subsidies, but their efforts at cost-containment are no better, and in many cases much worse, than private colleges simply because of the politics involved. Publics have a much larger tax base to rely on than do privates. As a consequence of this important distinction, a few private colleges have closed their doors or have taken drastic steps to avoid closing. But that is a fate that does not occur to publics even if their financial management is weak. Peter Drucker probably said it best of all:

> **Unless challenged, every organization tends to become slack, easygoing, diffuse.**

Our colleges are not immune from this indictment. On the contrary, we exemplify it in many ways. Being lean, fit, and trim are not in vogue. Cost containment is seen as a sign of weakness, so we throw money at our problems rather than make tough choices consistent with our mission. Since the money is not ours, throwing it around is not a primary concern. We can peddle quality, and everyone is brainwashed into believing that quality comes at a phenomenally high cost.

> **Like a French chef, we make tasty pastry and spill a lot of cream in the process.**

During the mid-1960s and early 1970s, we earned the disrespect of the nation because we could not control our campuses. They were called student protests – even riots. But we were not well-versed in handling such untoward events, be they riots or disturbances; indeed, freedom of action and freedom of expression were always the cornerstone of our campuses, so we allowed the disturbances more and more leeway until too late we realized that they were suffocating the very freedom we were honor-bound to defend. We now face the same disrespect because of our inability to control our costs; and in the process we jeopardize the very system that has served us well and was the envy of the world.

It is worth repeating; the public does not want more reasons for the inordinate increases, the dallying around, the hollow promises, the ceaseless repetition of unmet expectations, and the continuation of a once-respected endeavor that has slowly, but surely focused on its own welfare. The public understands that the cost of most things will go up over time. But not at usury rates.

The next two chapters give the real reasons why college costs have become outlandish.

Meager Faculty Teaching Loads

I started working at State University one year ago as an academic advisor in the School of Education. Although my five children and myself are college graduates, I was totally unaware of university procedures, and as a parent, grandparent, and taxpayer, I totally resent full-time faculty members with class loads of two classes one semester and sometimes three classes the next semester.

The writer is a nonteaching employee of a large public university and is expressing a universal outrage at the scant teaching loads enjoyed by many of our professors. This particular university is not alone; many of our institutions, large and small, public and private, have inadequate teaching loads. Which leads us to better understand one of the major reasons why the cost of higher education got so high. The other reason is the increasing bloat at every level of the administration.

Before we examine the faculty workload a little more closely, the typical college budget should be explained to a degree that is understood by the average person. While colleges differ in many respects, they all have budgets that support a large number of people; all colleges and universities are labor-intensive. They always were, and remain, places where people, not machines, predominate. And this is true even where computers hold sway and online courses are used. Whether teaching, administering, providing support services, cleaning lab equipment, or cutting the grass, we use a lot of people to do a vast array of jobs. Even as computer technology was touted as a labor-saving device – and in a convoluted way, it is – we have all added more staff to keep up with the ever-changing technology and to keep the systems running properly.

Our faculty are, or should be, the single biggest category of people on any college campus, although there are institutions where nonteaching staff are now rivaling the number of professors. While there may be slight differences depending on the institution, our faculty consume anywhere from 35 to 50 percent of the college budget. The rest of the workforce will use from 25 to 30 percent.

Beyond any doubt, colleges are labor-intensive organizations. The main drivers of cost are the direct educational expenses for faculty and the academic services that support teaching. The following chart indicates that instruction and student services comprise 85 to 87 percent of the total expenditures for the average four-year public institution and community college. The proportion for private institutions is about 70 percent, primarily because those schools award significantly more financial aid money – around 20 percent of their total expenses. Bottom line, whether the money comes from tuition, taxes, or endowments, colleges and universities spend, on average, 75 percent of their operating budgets on personnel expenses, including benefits, according to Robert Dickeson, senior vice president of Lumina Foundation for Education.

Average Percentage of College Budgets Spent on Instruction and Student Services

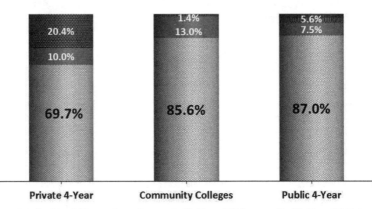

Source: National Association of College and University Business Officers

The average professor in 1988–89 was paid about $32,000 with an additional 20 percent of that, about $6,400, for fringe benefits. Today it is well over $85,000, with some professors getting over $200,000 as a base teaching salary. Really generous retirement benefits (10– 11 percent), along with medical, dental, and vision insurances are additional and are provided at most colleges. It should be emphasized that professors, in general, have worked hard to get tenure and to improve their rank, and most importantly, they are capable of doing a good job. Most of them have earned a doctorate or have other credentials that are impressive, all of which takes considerable effort, time, energy, and brain power. They are well-prepared to teach and conduct scholarship, and their compensation is not extravagant.

The problem is not salary; it is that far too many of our professors teach too little and blame it on a host of "intrusions" such as research, committee work, preparation, advising students, and anything else that will get them out of the classroom. It is one of academia's not so small ironies that we all went into this line of work to teach; we were enthusiastic to get before a class and excited about influencing college students and sharing our expertise with them. And as the years went by, we developed every reason in the book to get out of teaching. We became very clever at it, so much so that many professors teach little or nothing at all.

A professor who had just retired wrote to tell me that he had taught in major universities and small colleges, private and public. When he started, he taught 15 credits per semester and he published eight books. During his last years, his teaching load was reduced to six credits per semester and his publishing ceased. He pointed out that there were professors at his last university who taught no courses. He went on to say that his university (a large state university), if audited, would report a nine-credit teaching load for its faculty. "But," to use his words, "that is by a rather dishonest system of counting three-hour courses as 4.5 if there are more than 30 students and double if there are graduate students. Serving on committees earns points, as does every thesis and dissertation. But, many professors want to get out of directing such things as well as teaching."

It is a sorry state of affairs when our college teachers earn points and are rewarded for those points by having less teaching. And that is the point that is hard to explain – the unending struggle to reduce the teaching load or find some way to get out of the classroom when the initial lure of the profession was to teach and remain an active scholar. In what has to be one of the more bizarre cases, a professor earned an overload teaching stipend yet taught no courses. It went as follows: His normal teaching load was 12 credits, but because he was a full professor, he received a three-credit reduction, bringing his workload to nine credit hours. He was chairman of a department, so he received a six-credit reduction; he served on two committees, each of which called for a three-credit reduction, thereby giving him a 15-credit reduction on a base of 12. For this he was paid for a three-credit teaching overload without setting foot in the classroom.

This case should not be considered normal or common. What it serves to point out is that whatever the "official" teaching load is, there are countless ways to get around it. You can be assured that anyone trying to determine the teaching workload of the faculty at the above institution would be left with the belief that 12 credits was the correct number. Wrong! At this institution, and at many others where reduced teaching loads are a common occurrence, the myth continues that the official version and reality are the same. What is also instructive about this admittedly uncommon example is the state of mind or attitude fostered at so many of our institutions that anything and almost everything is more important than teaching.

The message is loud and clear: Your teaching load will be reduced if you engage in other activities. Or to put it more accurately, teaching is at the bottom of the totem pole. A piece of scholarship gets you out of the classroom. So does a special committee, an assignment of some kind, longevity, high faculty rank, or being the head of a self-designed program.

The latest activity to get the faculty out of the classroom is the specialty institute. This is where a faculty member develops a special expertise in some academic specialty that is not part of a department.

Women's studies is a good example, or foreign studies, or whatever a faculty member can get approved by the president. Whoever designs the program and becomes its director can expect a reduced teaching load. These special programs abound on most campuses, and are usually the delight of the instituting faculty member. But what kind of message does it send to our students, and more importantly, what kind of introduction does it give our new, bright faculty who initially didn't aim to be college teachers so they could then get out of teaching.

In case you are wondering why a full professor should have gotten a three-credit reduction, as in the case mentioned above, it was because there was a perception that full professors need more time to do all the research they do. Yet there is no evidence to support this contention. Indeed, one could make an argument that young assistant professors trying to earn tenure and promotion are more apt to publish than are full professors who have "paid their dues." In a cursory survey I did years ago to determine who did more scholarship among a faculty that numbered 350, liberally counting almost anything that was written or given in academic conferences, scholarship turned out to be fairly evenly distributed among all four ranks, instructor through full professor. But – surprise of surprises – those in academic administration who put in daily 9 to 5 hours doing administrative work pumped out just as much as our nine-credit teaching faculty members.

Research is given as the primary reason why faculty are out of the classroom, and some faculty do great research. Because of the time it demands, they ought to teach fewer hours. But to blithely assume that because a few of the nation's over 450,000 private and public college and university faculty members are capable of doing seminal research and are producing worthwhile results, all college faculty ought to teach fewer hours is to take advantage of the system, and it is driving costs upward at an outrageous rate.

In my own state of Pennsylvania, one public university claims its faculty teach only nine or fewer hours per semester because of their heavy research commitment, yet hundreds upon hundreds of them teach at two-year campuses where the libraries cannot sustain creditable research that deserves a nine-credit load. Nor do they have the labs or other facilities needed for seminal research. And to add a little insult to the whole charade, the faculty teach only nine credits of freshman- and sophomore-level work because these are two-year programs. These are not high-powered academic programs that require intensive and extraordinary preparation. They are essentially two-year colleges where the teaching load should be 15 hours per semester, but it is only nine.

Keep in mind that 60 percent of all college faculty members have never written or even edited a book, and 32 percent have never published one journal article. And many of those who have published stop doing it after a while. Yet the low teaching loads continue. In Richard Louv's "Eduflation" article, he wrote about the relatively highly paid professor who was now relaxing, though still on the payroll, because he had paid his dues. This may be considered by some to be hard-hitting or an isolated example (which it is not), but it is in no way as hard-hitting or penetrating as Prof. Peter Drucker's article titled "The Professor as Featherbedder." Listen to this ringing indictment of a very revered group:

> **By the time faculty members reach their early or mid-40s, they typically have been in academic life for 20 years – and typically have not worked in any other environment. Most faculty members, by that time, have done all the research and have written all the books they will ever write. Beyond that age, only a very small number of first-rate people remain productive. To be sure, these scholars and teachers who continue to produce are the people of whom everybody thinks when talking of historians, anthropologists, or metallurgists, but their number is very small indeed. The rest have, in effect, retired into boredom. They know their stuff, but they are no longer excited by it. They need a different environment, a different challenge, a different career. They need to be "repotted." This middle-aged faculty member is far from burned out. But he is bored. And the common remedies — to get a divorce and take up with a 19-year-old undergraduate; to take to the bottle; to take to the psychoanalyst's couch — don't cure the disease. And unless this competent, but bored person finds a new challenge, a new environment, and different work and different colleagues, irreversible deterioration sets in.**

A harsh indictment by Professor Drucker, but not far off the mark, and even though it was written in 1979, it applies even more so today. We all have observed some of the boredom, some of the playing around, some of the bottle-nipping, but not always to the degree Professor Drucker relates. What we have observed is that the excitement of teaching decreases for many, along with anything but a pretense of real scholarship. So the desire to be in the classroom diminishes as the clamor to improve quality by teaching less becomes more strident. We have also observed that a temporary change of environment, as with a paid sabbatical, is not always the rejuvenator it is advertised to be. For those who accomplish significant scholarship, it is; for those who posture and pretend, however, it is a break from a boring situation that does not really improve upon return.

It is worth expounding upon the true story mentioned earlier. While discussing this manuscript at a local restaurant, the authors chatted with a professor who walked by and was still teaching at the college we had worked. During our conversation he told us of his travel plans, his vacation schedule, and his work schedule. He had decided that his dues had been paid. His schedule of teaching was now set at Tuesdays and Thursday, and he reminded us of the many breaks in the academic year: fall break, month long semester break, spring break, and really short semesters. Then with absolutely no recognition of how bizarre it sounded, he spelled out for us how much he was now entitled to drift along at the very margins of professionalism. When he left, I said to my colleague, "He has the impression that he was a stoker working in the depths of a ship for 40 years, and finally now has a breath of fresh air."

This is more than a perfect example; it is unfortunately a common example. Far too many professors, under the guise of *professionalism*, are able to set their own hours, their own boundaries, and their own self-regard prior to consideration of their responsibilities to their field of endeavor and their constituency. Indeed, just about all other professions: medical doctors, dentists, lawyers, etc. have constraints that call for responsibility, boundaries, and accountability. Even artists in all fields of the arts are accountable to their various publics. Most professions also require constant renewal of skills by way of mandatory updating within the field of expertise. Professors, once rank and tenure are achieved, set their own individual standard of achievement, advancement, and accommodation. Some do it well, too many feel "it is now time to reap the rewards of a life too hard-pushed."

The authors realize these are harsh indictments of professors everywhere. We readily acknowledge there are many professors who do not fit the category of laggard. We have seen them and have worked closely with them. And we applaud their efforts which continue by virtue of their own sense of work ethics, and by virtue of what can truly be called true professionalism. However, far too many do fit the description of laggard.

> **College professors are not overpaid,**
> **they are terribly underworked.**

Let me make a comparison that is anathema to most college professors. Public high school teachers teach 20 to 30 hours per week, an average of about 25. This means they teach five classes five days a week; many teach as many as six classes five days a week. Many of our professors teach nine hours over the same week, which means three classes that meet only three days a week. Some professors arrange a two-day-a-week schedule, which comes to 4½ hours of teaching for only two days. Many more teach only two classes per semester, which brings them into the classroom a total of six hours per week. What do they do with the rest of their time?

The professors will say they need a lot of time to prepare for their courses, with the implication that high school teachers do not. The professors will say their subjects are tougher, yet not one of them would switch places with a high school teacher. And for good reason. The professor has few or no discipline problems; the high school teacher probably does, and most certainly will have some student problems if it is an inner-city school. The professor makes on average one-third more than the high school teacher and has higher-functioning academic students, which in and of itself is more rewarding; the high school teacher must teach all who live in the district, bright or not so bright, civil or rude, stable or not so stable, and in an environment that, generally speaking, cannot compare with that of your typical college.

Not only do the professors have a substantially shorter work week, they also have a shorter school year. Over the years, the academic year for colleges has shrunk by two weeks on many college campuses. Forty years ago a semester was 17 weeks; today it is 15 weeks, including a week for finals. Some colleges have even cut that to 13 weeks with a week for finals. However, ask any student who may be taking the normal load of five courses whether he or she had five finals. Chances are a professor or two decided to eliminate the final. Again, we are not questioning the professor's right to decide such academic matters. The point is simply that the professor's total workload is in constant remission. It's very much like the auto industry making some cars smaller and jacking the price up, or the full-length fur coat that is now half length, while the price keeps going up.

A former governor of Missouri has seen the problem grow to the point where he says today's college students receive a semester and a half less instruction than students did in the 1940s. Is it any wonder that professors do not like to be compared to high school teachers? It's a topsy-turvy educational world. Those who have the higher salary and the better conditions get to work less than those who put in a very demanding day filled with the stressful uncertainty of a widely diverse range of student abilities and backgrounds.

Surveys have been done to try to ascertain the hours worked per week by the average professor. They show 50 to 60 hours per week, but the survey methodology has its shortcomings and is very suspect. Asking the professors to fill out the forms describing their nonteaching workloads does not build one's confidence in the scientific method; quite frankly, it is very self-serving. It would be much like allowing the average citizen to decide when he has paid enough taxes. Forget the reporting and forget the audits. Just let all people decide how much they should pay in taxes, and take their word as gospel. An astute observer of the higher education scene and former high-ranking official in the U.S. Department of Education, Chester Finn, had this to say about faculty workloads:

> **A great many faculty do very little work, at least on behalf of the institutions that pay their salaries. Although practically all of them appear to think they do an enormous amount - certainly they assert that they do, the basis for these self-estimates is a set of norms that practically nobody outside the academy would credit.**

However, for those who place even a modicum of trust in self-reported estimates of time spent on professional responsibilities, the following chart indicates the proportion of full-time faculty reporting they spent nine hours or more per week teaching was 43.6 percent in 2010, down from 63.4 percent two decades ago and 56.5 percent just 10 years ago, according to a national survey of faculty conducted every three years by the Higher Education Research Institute. The research study, which is based on responses from 23,824 faculty members across the country, further concludes that the decline in scheduled faculty teaching hours is mirrored by a corresponding decrease in overall time spent in preparation for teaching.

Percentage of Full-Time Faculty Teaching 9 or More Hours Per Week

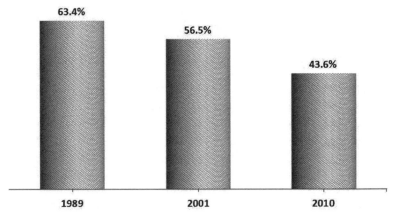

Source: Higher Education Research Institute at UCLA

What should a standard teaching load be at a four-year college? If the American Association of University Professors (AAUP) national office is to be believed, it should be nine hours. But their credibility has been shaken and is sharply reduced from the time when they fought for real principles such as academic freedom and due process. Now they engage in building union membership and reducing workloads. And as any good union mentality dictates, membership at any cost is important, second only to conformity. So they put forth the argument that nine credits is an adequate workload, paying no attention to the fact that many professors are not into research, and others are publishing less than first-rate stuff.

Quite frankly, the AAUP is fearful of discriminating between those few who deserve a reduction in teaching because of seminal research and those many who ought to be in the classroom more. That fear of discriminating, of not treating professionals as individuals, is the true mark of a union mentality and is partly responsible for the decline in productivity of the average faculty member.

Professor Jacques Barzun, a giant in the world of academia who has written great books including the highly respected *The Art of Teaching* – all while teaching 15 credits each semester – is not fearful of discriminating between important research and trivial stuff:

> **To suppose that every owner of a Ph.D. can carry on valuable research while also teaching, and find time to write it up in publishable form, is contrary to fact. Motive and ability are not to be had on demand. Formerly a scholar who published did so for fame and the public good; now the objective is promotion and the survival of a young family.**

It brings us to the main point about research: some of it is very important; much of it isn't, beyond self-satisfaction, and even those in the field don't bother reading it because it represents a study, a survey, a preconceived idea that is jacked up by 200 questionnaires. If we wait a year or two, the thesis advocated will be reversed by someone else who sends out 200 questionnaires and with a 13 percent return rate is able to show contrary results. Some of it is interesting, much of it cannot be called real research, and the results are valuable to practically no one in academia, nor to posterity.

Countless published articles do not represent advancement of knowledge broadly defined. Nor do they represent progress in the sciences where a theory is explored either for its own sake or practical ends, or for advancement built upon the work of inquiring and eminently successful researchers. Many do not pose new philosophic theories or advance those of former intellectual giants. Rather, they are a compilation of data emanating from a hypothesis of such limited scope and value as to be ultimately confined to the dustbins of academic and intellectual irrelevancy.

And, even after such a severe indictment, we are not calling for a cessation of these academic efforts. Rather, no one should get reduced teaching for doing what was initially expected of them: good classroom teaching along with continued scholarship activities. The vast majority of us need to spend more time in the classroom while maintaining the sharpness of our subject, our scholarship, and our students. If we want to do research that is important in keeping academically sharp, and is of moderate interest, then we should do it within the confines of a 12-hour teaching load. Too quickly we forget that professors always taught far fewer courses than high school teachers (and for shorter ever-decreasing semesters) for exactly the reasons we now artificially magnify and lean on for even more teaching reductions.

Professor Barzun recalls an era a few decades ago when the college professor taught 10 courses a year, five each semester, and did research. No one is making a case for returning to that schedule, but it does serve to remind us that there were reasons, and good ones, for reducing the teaching load and thereby sharply distinguishing the college professor from the high school teacher. The teaching load was reduced to 12 hours each semester, thereby allowing more than adequate time for the average professor to stay active with scholarship, with publishing, and with most research. When it went below 12 hours each semester, we took advantage of the system and initiated a sustained period of self-indulgence – both financially and academically. Far too many colleges have a teaching load of nine hours, and many more a teaching load of six or even three hours each semester.

These are all "official" loads, meaning that if you were to call your local state university or your high-profile private university and ask what the faculty workload is at their institution, they would probably say nine or perhaps six hours per semester. A few might even say 12 hours each semester. What they won't tell you is that the actual teaching load is lower than the official load for a variety of reasons, reductions being one of them.

Another reason may be that a course had just a few students in it, and rather than make waves and cancel it, the professor would be allowed to teach it as a tutorial, meaning he could meet with the two or three students in his office a few times and call it a full course. Not that tutorials are bad – on the contrary, some real learning can and does go on in them. But the assignment of a full course to the professor when there are so few students is a financially derelict and unethical action. It may serve the institution well when those in charge are asked about its "official teaching load," but it is a deception that drives the costs of a college education higher and higher, beyond reasonable increases. In their very detailed work, Thomas P. Snyder and Eva C. Galambox reported a decline in teaching load from an average of 10.2 semester hours over the academic year in 1980 to 8.4 semester hours just five years later. Put another way that is a 17.6 percent decline in productivity between 1980 and 1985. Is it any wonder tuition skyrocketed during this period?

Could any business or endeavor maintain any semblance of cost control with declines in productivity like that? Their work also pointed out that just about every position that combined administration and teaching – e.g., deans, chairmen, directors, etc. – also experienced steep declines in the teaching side of their responsibility. Only the position of assistant dean increased substantially from an average of 5.1 semester hours to 7.2 hours of teaching. As mentioned, reduced time is not the only way to get out of the classroom. One can have assistants fill in for the prof or, on any given day, one may find a note on the classroom door that classes will not meet because the professor is off to a seminar, workshop, or any other contrivance that will take him or her away. No one yet is able to explain why all these academic conferences, seminars, and workshops occur during the academic year. They could just as well occur during the 3½-month summer break, or during the four-week semester break.

Let us interject at this point that the vast majority of professors are excellent teachers and lecturers and, as a group, have always been outstanding in the classroom. Now and then we hear complaints about the direction of their politics or the new subjects they are teaching, but in our combined experience of more than 85 years with higher education and professors, it is valid to say they are usually at their best in the classroom. Even those who cry the loudest for reduced teaching do not lower the quality of their teaching. Nonetheless, it has to be repeated over and over ... most are woefully underworked.

Where does the ultimate responsibility lie for such low teaching loads for faculty members? Who makes the final decision allowing the workload to go from twelve to nine to six to three hours per semester? The legal answer is the board of trustees in just about all of our private colleges, and in the public colleges that are not unionized. Where unionization exists, the workload is up for negotiations. But in both cases *the president* is the main force for determining the final outcome.

Through initiative, direction, willpower, and straightforward leadership, the president is the one who makes the final recommendations to the board. If he or she is inclined to be persuaded, then that will be the course taken. If the president fears a vote of no confidence from the faculty, then reductions can result.

Some years ago, the faculty of New York University voted to make all three-credit courses four credits. Now, one would think that they would add some time onto the classroom sessions commensurate with the credit increase, but they did not. The classes meet for the same three hours per week, the students have to pay for the four credits rather than three, and of course, the professors had their "officially" stated teaching load increased by 33½ percent without doing one bit more teaching. Perhaps they talked faster to give the semblance of more value received for more money paid, or perhaps they assigned more homework. It really doesn't matter how one justifies these antics which the president signed off on, as did the trustees. No one bothered to complain, and we in academia answer to no one when questionable maneuvers such as these take place. At this same private university, the graduate courses that formerly met two hours for three credits are now meeting two hours for four credits. It's a Faustian bargain no one wanted to miss.

The University of New Hampshire did the same thing, and not a peep came out of the state legislature. If a student paid for a full car and got only three wheels instead of four, you can bet everyone would hear about it. Yet they'll pay for four credits and receive only three credits of teaching time, and no one issues a protest. Blaming the students is the lesser part of the problem. It is the faculty and the administration, along with the trustees of the institution, who deserve the opprobrium.

Small private colleges are just as adept at getting their faculty in front of a minimum number of students. A vice president of finance of just such a college told me, with pride in his voice, that the faculty at his college taught only nine credits, and each of their classes averaged only eight students. When I suggested that a lot of creative and seminal research must be going on, his demeanor changed in the way one reacts to a question that has broken an unspoken role of protocol. His subdued response was to the effect that he hadn't seen all that much.

Since there is usually a difference between the official version of a teaching load and the real one, we must have a teaching load audit of randomly chosen colleges, public and private. Since audits are conducted on defense plants, hospitals, and any other businesses and agencies that benefit from our tax largess, why not a teaching audit at our higher education institutions, which consume so much of our public monies and have brought into question our public trust? The audit need not be complicated and would review only teaching workload, not other scholarly activities. What we would probably find out is:

About 10 percent of the full-time faculty were on paid sabbatical for one or both semesters, and therefore taught no students. Additionally, whatever the official teaching load the institution states, a number of faculty members will have fewer courses because of reductions due to a variety of reasons. A 12-credit load became a nine- or six-credit load; a nine-credit load became a six or three-credit load. A few of the reductions may be justifiable; most are not. But justification of reductions is not the point of the audit – rather, the variance between reality and official version is the reason.

Some of the courses would have an amazingly small number of students who received grades. At this point I should explain why the grade roster that comes out at the end of the semester is of importance in our audit and not the enrollment roster that comes out prior to the first day of classes. Just about every class loses a handful of students as the semester progresses. Some lose more than others – here we think of our early morning classes ... some students like to sleep in ... enough said! Some professors start with 15 students, but after the first week are down to 12. That's why we have a withdrawal period, and every grade of W is one less student the faculty teaches and grades.

Our audit would show that some of our faculty members end the semester with very small classes. This is often not the fault of the professor, but in determining the size of a class, its initial size measured against what we know will be its final size should be a definite consideration in determining whether or not a full course is assigned to a professor; or perhaps it should be a tutorial or an independent study, and neither should be counted as a full course. Some of the courses would have an amazingly large number of students, in the hundreds; then the question should be raised as to who taught and evaluated the students – a faculty member or a graduate assistant or two?

To get the real teaching load of the entire university, one would have to slog through some murky waters with labs, graduate courses, and a pile of other debris that serves to obscure the count. But it is possible, and if done by one who persists and asks the right questions, the final number would no doubt surprise even administrators who are protective of the official version. Having done this once at a relatively large institution, we were all surprised, including the faculty, at just how much teaching reduction had accrued over the years. A course less for this, another for that, and the end result was that about one-third of the official teaching load was not being taught by the professor who was supposed to teach the requisite number of courses.

Reduced teaching, or released time, as it is called, is not a natural phenomenon. Released time from teaching is the result of a systemic or organizational laziness that slowly envelopes individuals as they spend more and more time with their older colleagues. It is almost a conspiracy leading toward and often resulting in idleness. Those who defend released time assume that it will strengthen the program and the college, although they are unable to offer even a hint of confirmation that such an assumption is true. By having a released time program, goes the argument, we can show the world our commitment to excellence. However, there is no real evidence that shows released time contributes to anything except a lower teaching load. Dr. Robert Boice, the director of the Center for Faculty Development at California State University, Long Beach, has conducted research on the subject of released time and has concluded that:

1. verified assessments of normal workloads contradicted faculty claims of being too busy for additional scholarship;
2. faculty given released time usually persisted in old habits;
3. new faculty showed no obvious benefits of a typical released time program; and
4. faculty in released time programs verbalized real doubts about how to use extra time for meaningful scholarship.

At the very least, the value derived from released time is questionable to a very serious degree, yet the practice is widespread and increases the cost of higher education by a tremendous amount. From a productivity standpoint, a faculty member whose workload drops from twelve to nine credits has achieved a dubious 25 percent reduction in productivity. For someone to drop from nine credits to six, the reduction in productivity is a sizable 33⅓. In the business world, increases in productivity (and dreaded decreases) are measured in 1 and 2 percentage points, even fractions of a point. But then again, we are all too oft reminded that colleges are not businesses. And in a way, they are not; they are educational institutions generally not designed for profit. In spite of this, they should all be run in a businesslike way, which is often not the case. From a former professor and international civil servant come these words:

The sad thing is that professors don't believe what universities teach in elementary economics: if productivity increases, real income will increase.

What better example of this than one of the top management schools in the entire country, located at MIT. It had a dean, a deputy dean, a senior associate dean, two associate deans, three department heads, and a director of finance and administration running the place. It had 43 full professors, 21 associate professors, 24 assistant professors, 21 lecturers, and three adjunct professors teaching a total of 103 undergraduate students, 212 graduate students, and 151 others. That is quite a student/faculty ratio, guided by a top-heavy administration. It serves to point out another of the many ironies in higher education: This management school is known for teaching its students the benefits of productivity, finance, organization, economics, and pricing, among other things – all things that should convince anyone that productivity and cost benefits are important and not just a classroom exercise.

This example is a good one because it leads to a rather ostensive contradiction. Because of the prominence of these schools of business administration, many of the professors are able to command large salaries for their work in the school, along with large consulting fees for their work outside of the school. In a perverse way, their academic prominence allows them to be less productive with their teaching load so that they can be more productive with off-campus activities that net them extra dollars. In his book, *The Empire Builders*, author J. Paul Mark points out that one professor in another very highly regarded business school started his own company that specialized in consultation work. He employed more than 100 professionals, and his work on company business often kept him away from his college office for prolonged stretches of time.

The author goes on to say that teaching ability is not emphasized or even required, and several full professors have not set foot in a classroom for years. The dean of the school was absent for weeks at a time, which did not seem to bother the faculty at all. Indeed, a majority of the tenured members had private businesses on the side and liked the idea of being free of much monitoring from anyone. It is no wonder the dean was absent; he sat on the boards of eight very large public companies, each of which met for one or two days each month.

If an institution were to be asked if it has a policy concerning outside work, the stock answer would be, "Of course." Then the policy would be shown with something approximating one day a week allowed for outside work. Does anyone keep track? Of course not. "We are dealing with professionals!" is the answer. We are supposed to accept this just as we do the professor's notion of the number of hours he or she works each week. Maybe the IRS should designate all professionals, of every stripe, as self-determinates for the amount of taxes they pay. No verification necessary.

There was a time, not so long ago, when high-powered professors and deans would obtain grants to underwrite their research and thus allow them to give outside governmental agencies and businesses the benefits of their expertise. The grant would come to the university, which would distribute it in a fair fashion – some for overhead, some for the professor's research, some for the financial well-being of the educational institution and the department from which the research emanated. If the grant came from a private company, it could be deducted as a charitable contribution to a nonprofit institution, or it could be charged as a legitimate business expense. The method of deduction makes little difference to the company from a financial point of view. But, reasoned some financially astute professors, if we started our own company, we could trade on the connection we have with our prestigious university while cutting it out of being middle man. The grant ceases to be a grant to the university and becomes an expense payment made directly to the professor's private company, thereby preserving more profits for the professor.

Back to release time. If it is given, it should be given only for the period during which the research is being conducted. Too often released time is given, and when the research ends or the book is written, the released time from teaching continues. Maybe we ought to admit that some professors are good scholars and teachers, but are incapable of producing advanced research that is sufficiently weighty enough to receive, if not high acclaim, at least worthy recognition from one's peers throughout the country. Scholarship can occur without publication, and that should be recognized as a positive factor without the onus of "publish or perish." It certainly should not result in released time. Let us not forget the two 14-week semesters, along with the sizable semester break and some smaller breaks interspersed throughout, and we can easily conclude that the higher educational school year leaves ample time for scholarship at a variety of levels.

Add to this the almost universal practice of sabbaticals every seven years or so, whereby professors can become immersed in their research for a paid extended period of time. Incidentally, Connecticut College, along with a few others, has reduced the seventh-year paid sabbatical to every four years. That eliminates three years of teaching between sabbaticals, which pushes to an extreme level the inability of comprehension by the paying family and the general public. There are other reasons too as to why the standard teaching workload ought to be 12 credits. One of the most important is that teaching and scholarship go hand-in-hand. The fact is that far too many universities, now joined by numerous small high-cost colleges, wish to be known as "research institutions." The obvious reason for this is that less teaching will occur at these places. The long-held belief that research, and scholarship in general, can help inspire good teaching is losing ground.

Why has released time come into being? Why have faculty teaching workloads, in general, become lighter and lighter over the years? The reduction recognizes the complaints of faculty, who bemoan what they consider to be work overloads. And it is promoted as a purported curative for burnout. But the main reason is because just about all of our prestigious colleges (a small minority of all colleges) started the trend because they felt they had an elite status, and their particular public could afford to pay the increased going rate. The majority of the remaining colleges, which ordinarily looked to the elite for academic direction, followed with reduced teaching loads, along with the ever increasing costs to students, parents, and supporting government.

Reduced teaching loads are attractive, no doubt about it, but they may also be counterproductive and ineffective. They result in circular reasoning, implying that since reduced teaching provides the faculty with even more self-directed goals, then the program must be effective. By offering a program of reduced teaching, the college or university is making a powerful statement about campus values in terms of research. But this is erroneous thinking and is self-serving, since no lasting changes are made by the faculty who receive the reduced teaching loads.

In research done by Prof, Robert Boice and published as far back as 1987, titled "Is Released Time an Effective Component of Faculty Development Programs?" not only were "the accomplishments often small, and often what might have been expected in the ordinary course of a faculty member's carrying out of responsibilities, [but] grants seem to go first to those already teaching at a high level. Such faculty members are also likely to participate in various opportunities for faculty development whether stipends (or released time) were attached or not." This statement actually came from the work of Eble and McKeachie, done in 1985. Also, work done by Creswell in 1985 and reported in Prof. Boice's article would confirm the unscientific survey I conducted and described earlier on in which full professors were given a three-credit reduction from teaching because it was assumed they do more research than do lower ranked professors, but in fact, they did not. Creswell stated:

> **A favorite premise in awarding released time is this: faculty need time, especially from demands such as teaching, to show improvements in productivity. But relevant evidence suggests that productive faculty surpass other colleagues in finding ways to make time for research and writing. The factor that predicts productivity seems to be individual patterns (such as habit of regular writing) that begin early in careers.**

It is clear that the idea that faculty need reduced teaching is a myth encouraged by organizations such as the national AAUP and perpetuated by the faculty. Creswell in 1985 also reported that it is not necessarily true that faculty who are productive in research must sacrifice essential time in teaching. They are not mutually exclusive, as some faculty would have us believe. One of the real problems associated with reduced teaching, in addition to the unnecessary financial burden it puts on students and their families, is the message it sends to everyone: teaching is secondary to scholarship; teaching is of lesser value than other academic endeavors; teaching is not very important; even committee work is more important.

This kind of thinking results in good teachers re-evaluating their priorities simply because it is no badge of merit to be doing what you are good at if its rank in the hierarchy of academic values is low. It must be emphasized that at the college level, both teaching and scholarship are important, and as higher education moves from imparting information to generating new information, we should value both teaching and scholarship, and strive to draw a balance between the two, which, at the present time, is seriously out of balance.

Another reason given to justify reduced teaching loads is committee work. Many faculty wallow in this excuse, which is not to say that committee work is not important; rather, it should never be used to reduce a professor's classroom teaching. Yet, some colleges will selectively cut a faculty member's teaching load when he or she is serving on a committee or two. Of course it takes time to serve on committees, but there is more than enough time to participate in appropriate committee work even with the 12-hour teaching load. Committees started out for good reason: college faculty members needed to determine the best curriculum to offer their students; they needed to screen the best applicants to teach the prescribed curriculum; and they needed to deal with a host of other important academic matters. In a very real sense, the professors are the academic officers of the institution and should have a lot to say about the academic side of a college. Academic governance is the title given to this whole process that involves faculty in virtually all aspects of academic life on campus. It is needed, it is important, and it is one of the original reasons given for why professors teach less than their high school counterparts.

The role of faculty members on just about all colleges has changed over the last five or six decades. No longer do faculty dine with students very often; no longer do faculty engage themselves in the daily life of the college, including dorm life; no longer do faculty get involved with many of the very personal decisions that students face. In loco parentis fell by the wayside. In 1971 it was decided that the age of adulthood should be lowered from 21 to 18 years. Increased financial aid from government sources has brought more complex regulation. Higher security called for more professional assistance. Liability increased. Dorm living became more varied, as did food service. The need for faculty committees staffed by professors with deep expertise in linguistics or chemistry, who were very useful in less complex times, is less so today. Faculty governance gave way to academic governance. Committee work directed at the nonacademic side need not take so much time. It places some faculty members who are top-notch teachers and scholars in their field in the position of trying to influence dormitory safety regulations or some other nonacademic aspect of college life that is entirely foreign to their training or ability.

Faculty governance, as opposed to academic governance, is often an antagonistic and time-consuming struggle between the faculty (or a group of very vocal faculty) and the administration. It becomes a device whereby the faculty challenge the administration on just about any and all matters, whether or not they pertain to academics. It is time-consuming, does nothing for general morale, and is costly in terms of the unnecessary work involved, resulting in attempts to justify less teaching so that more committee work can replace it.

The authors of a very brief article espousing the growth of faculty governance described it as "a support system committed to progress through collegial rather than adversarial strategies." This appears to be a very laudable goal. However, just five paragraphs later they state: "An alarming percentage find themselves overmatched and outwitted by administrators long on quick-fix management strategies but short on long-term effective policies and practices." Only an illogical mind can fail to grasp the intrinsic contradiction of these two opposing ideas. In a stinging assessment of committee work published in the National Center for the Study of Collective Bargaining in Higher Education and the Professions, Prof. Myron Lieberman of Ohio University observed:

Chapter 2

From the rhetoric of higher education, one would think that academicians are grievously overworked. Actually, a significant proportion of faculty time is devoted to collective decision-making, often on the trivial issues. Even when issues are resolved by individual decisions, there must frequently be a prior collective decision to delegate the decision to the individual. Despite the fact that they teach only three to nine hours a week, most professors do not conduct any meaningful research. It is, therefore, essential for most to find another justification for their lack of productivity; faculty self-governance meets this need very nicely, since its demands can be interpreted expansively and implemented with minimal effort and no accountability.

He goes on to say:

I don't want to participate in transportation policy. I just want to get where I'm going in a minimum amount of time and with convenience. I don't want to participate in making medical policy, I just want to be healthy, and if I need help, to get it promptly. But it's only in higher education that we've turned this around and made participation the end in a sense rather than simply the means which we should do our utmost to do without.

Call it what you will, committee work has assumed a greater control of our academic institutions than originally intended. As an example of faculty governance in action, I give a verbatim account sent to me by the dean of a highly recognized small private college in the middle-north part of our country:

Concerning faculty load, our situation may be interesting to you. The myth which animates official life here holds that faculty, although they teach only seven sections per year (three terms of 11 weeks each) and enjoy a very generous sabbatical policy, are "overworked." The heavy burden allegedly takes the form of such myriad related functions as scholarship, advising, committee work, and such. What no one mentions openly is that a) many faculty restrict themselves (as is their right) to a minimum of these functions, and b) many of these functions derive from the hyper-process bias of schools who insist on managing their affairs almost totally via faculty governance. Schools like ours squander enormous talent, time, and energy at the feet of twin idols – participative process and adversarial faculty/administrative structure.

One instance of our profligacy has been an innocuous proposal to change from quarter terms to a semester system. The administration has judged that such a change would greatly assist such efforts as retention and overall efficiency, and many faculty also favored it for academic reasons. Thus, in 1980–81, a specially constituted Calendar Committee had spent an entire year shepherding a proposal through the governance apparatus. At long last, the proposal won by a single vote of the faculty, but our president, alas, decided that the majority was insufficient as a basis for change. Five fumbling years passed. The process of reformulating a new proposal fell to an all-university faculty Commission on the Academic Climate, which included a Sub-Committee on Calendar.

The Commission's work consumed a full year (1985–86), and the chief recommendation of its 86-page product, "An Agenda for Excellence," has been a proposal to change to semesters. (By the way, our college had used such a system up to 1966; we were not dealing with a radical idea here.) This proposal was duly debated for the entire fall term, which included an all-day retreat of the entire faculty to consider in detail the ramifications of any change department by department. (The debate studiously avoided administrative reasons for change; intrusion of these into a faculty process would constitute unforgivable bad form.)

Finally, anticlimax again attended the effort, as the proposal lost by a vote of 79 (including 8 students) to 74. Thus, about 175 people, including a group of bright administrators, had devoted seven years of high-priced and ostensibly serious effort, failing to accomplish what a three-person group of executive delegates in a normal organization could achieve in a few weeks. Such experiences feed a distorted attitude among academics in all but the most beleaguered institutions.

He concludes with the belief that such governance activities, albeit exhausting and inconclusive, are nevertheless supremely important to the faculty, for they exemplify process and faculty status at work. It is fair to say that this drawn-out example is typical on many of our campuses. The "heavy" load of committee work substantiates the notion that the process is what really counts. And since the process has no accountability attached to it, there are no measurement devices that committee members should worry about, hence everyone is comfortable. It also calls for less teaching, because there are only so many hours in the day; and if people spend so much time in committee work, or thinking about committee work, then there is less time available for teaching.

In summary, with a direct and uncomplicated analysis, what every economist will tell you is that if a large percentage of the workforce is allowed to reduce efforts which are directly tied to the main originator of the purse and the enterprise, then the costs will go up disproportionally.

Bloated College Administrations

We college presidents and we college administrators have our own counterpart of the faculty committee. It is the conference, the workshop, the seminar on how to be an effective manager, how to be a better administrator, how to deal with unions, how to lead; and it is the annual two-day conference of the AAPE, the UFAM, the AHHEE. Make up any set of letters (and capitalize them), and I'm sure there is an annual conference somewhere celebrating the existence of what the letters stand for. Administrators have enough conferences and higher education association meetings to attend that they can be away from their respective campuses for weeks on end.

In one brief period of about a month-and-a-half, a period of no special significance, we received some 38 invitations to national and regional conferences, symposiums, workshops and seminars, all directed to presidents and other upper-level administrators, all lasting a day to a week. Each of them would cost money in travel, hotels, fees, etc., and all of them would keep us away from the campus for some time. As with committee work for faculty, they are a weak substitute for doing one's primary job. In addition, we must have people in charge when we are away so often, consequently we create positions of provost, vice president, executive vice president, and a host of others at colleges both small and large.

Before we look into this proliferation of administrative positions, let me say a word more about conferences. They are not inexpensive and the total cost is almost always picked up by the college. And they have become a bit ludicrous. The letter invited assistants to the president to be involved in a growing network of presidents' assistants who were planning a three-day conference in San Diego in January. The usual reasons were given why such a newly-founded organization should begin yearly meetings: personal convenience, the meeting of colleagues, comparing notes, finding solace, and simply enjoying time together. Among the steering committee were: assistant to the president, special assistant to the president (evidently, a higher position than just plain assistant), and executive assistant to the president (higher yet). As colleges build bureaucracies, the inevitable conference helps to perpetuate the various levels of bureaucracy by bonding the newly-created positions in permanence and self-proclaimed importance.

Successfully matching the low teaching productivity of faculty is the high bureaucratic level of staffing at so many of our colleges, especially at our large public institutions, where they have developed it into an art form.

Do we have too many administrators at many of our institutions? You decide. At a community college in the Midwest, it took some digging, but the final tally showed that there were 770 full-time administrators following a concerted buildup of new positions. What is astounding about the number is that the buildup took place over the last decade even as student enrollment steadily declined and the number of full-time faculty also declined. Even worse is that the number of administrators now just about equals the number of faculty. At the University of Minnesota, the new president was stymied when he wanted to reduce administrative costs, but no one could tell him what the costs were. *The Wall Street Journal* of Dec. 29, 2012, reported that over the previous decade, the university had added more than 1,000 new administrators, many of whom are paid well over $200,000 per year. This was twice as large as the number of added professors and twice the growth of students.

An even more egregious example is the University of Pennsylvania, as reported by *The Philadelphia Inquirer* in a five-part series (March 31–April 4, 1996). During the 18-year period from 1975 to 1993, Penn's undergraduate enrollment grew by 28 percent, while during the same time frame, the university increased its faculty by 22 percent. However, nonteaching staff increased by 83 percent. Under the heading "What Is Wrong with This Picture?" they illustrate increased enrollment of 29 full-time students from 1980 to 1993, while during the same 13-year period, the school added *1,820* administrators and other nonteaching staff.

More recent data concerns Purdue, one of America's top-rated public universities. Tenure track faculty increased 12 percent from 2001 to 2010. Student enrollment increased 5 percent, while the number of administrators increased an astonishing 58 percent. One need not be an economist to wonder why the tuition over the same period rose from $1,400 to nearly $9,000. This is a mind-boggling rate that averages close to 23 percent a year, but then again, administrators do not come cheaply. We should remember that the CPI during these nine years was uniformly low. Most public universities will point to their State House and blame lower tax support for the outlandish tuition increases, without once mentioning the dramatic increases of personnel they have acquired. Students understand better than most the bureaucracy created by the hiring glut. Read the letter written by a student who was captive in a heavily administrated state system:

> **Is there really excess fat in Penn State's bureaucracy that could be cut to help prevent tuition increases? I'm sure there is, because I received a three-dollar refund ($3.06 to be exact) that required the involvement of at least five people, a two-part form, and took over two weeks to process. The refund procedure began on February 24, when the two-part form was typed by the person officially requesting the refund.**
>
> **Three days later my three-dollar refund was "recommended" for approval by a budget administrator. Final approval required the signatures of two untitled bureaucrats – one on the 3rd of March and another on March 4th. Then the two-part form was sent to the controller, where a check was finally issued on March 9th. This is just one example of the bureaucratic monster our tuition money feeds. It makes one wonder what kind of bureaucratic red tape is involved in refunding a larger amount of money. This is certainly the kind of bureaucratic fat that can be cut to help reduce tuition increases.**

He probably didn't realize that tuition was not the only part of the cost. The taxpayer was underwriting a much larger share of the waste than he was. The president of this same university informed the students well in advance that there would be a 5 percent tuition increase. He also explained that he was announcing the tuition much earlier than normal so that students could be prepared. "Of course, this 5 percent increase is predicated on us getting a 14 percent increase from the state legislature."

Between 1993 and 2007, total spending per student increased by 34.5 percent, according to a Goldwater Institute report based on

Department of Education data. The following chart shows that when broken down by category, increases in expenditures for instruction rose 39.3 percent, while spending on administration leaped an eye-popping 61.2 percent. The report concluded that large government subsidies for higher education facilitate administrative bloat by insulating students from the real costs.

Administrative Costs Increased Faster Than Any Other College Expenses, 1993-2007

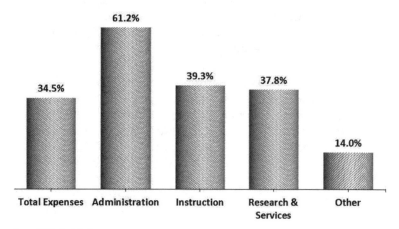

Source: Goldwater Institute

There is another disturbing trend documented by the Goldwater Institute study which shows that since the early 1990s, the number of full-time administrators per 100 students employed at American universities has soared 39% compared to the 18% increase in the number of instructors employed in teaching or research activities. Furthermore, the actual spending on administration-related expenditures per student lunged upwards by 66%. While overall higher education expenses rose 35% between 1993 -2007, administrative costs jumped a staggering 61% and instructional expenditures rose 39%.

During that same time period, Arizona State University increased the number of administrators per 100 students by 94 percent. Nearly one-half of all full-time employees at Arizona State are administrators. In 1975, colleges employed one administrator for every 84 students, and one professional staffer (admissions officers, information technology specialists, and the like) for every 50 students. By 2005, the administrator-to-student ratio grew to one administrator for every 68 students, while the ratio of professional staffers grew to one for every 21 students.

In their research, Martin and Hill arrived at similar conclusions. In their analysis of data on public research institutions dating from 1987 to 2008, they found a ratio of two full-time administrators for every one tenured or tenure-track faculty member. Over the same time, the number of tenure-track faculty per 100 students grew 3 percent while the executive and managerial staff grew by 9 percent. Mr. Martin concluded that "the balance between people who are actually in the trenches and those who are overseeing that work has gotten grossly out of line. That imbalance is one of the primary reasons why costs grew out of control over the last three decades."

> **A staggering statistic unearthed by a recent Wall Street Journal article revealed that the University of Minnesota employs one administrator for every 3½ students!**

The authors concluded that "Across U.S. higher education, nonclassroom costs have ballooned, administrative payrolls being a prime example. The number of employees hired by colleges and universities to manage or administer people, programs and regulations increased 50% faster than the number of instructors between 2001 and 2011, the U.S. Department of Education says. It's part of the reason that tuition, according to the Bureau of Labor Statistics, has risen even faster than health-care costs."

The proliferation of new administrative positions spurred a 28% surge in the higher education workforce from 2000 to 2012, according to a Delta Cost Project report entitled "Labor Intensive or Labor Expensive?" The report emphasizes that the sizeable increase in personnel costs is not related to instruction, but rather to student services that are not central to the missions of most colleges. The additional salaries are primarily connected to athletics, admissions, career counseling, psychological support services, and other non-academic activities.

> **Common sense tells us, very clearly, that large administrations are incubators for bureaucracies.**

In 1987, the governor of New York sent the huge State University of New York (SUNY) budget back to its preparers and said the increase asked for was unrealistic and certainly way out of line when compared to inflation. The SUNY Higher Education System was about the largest in the country with more than 186,000 full and part-time students and a staff that is unimaginably large. Its budget was $2.38 billion in 1987. The governor asked SUNY to review the budget and list items that could be excluded, thereby resulting in a more modest increase. After review, they could not find even one item to scratch. In 1988, the SUNY system was once again creaming the competition with its financial requests. It submitted a budget with an unbelievably large increase, and once again the governor was shaking his head. The requested 1989 budget was $2.6 billion, a 9.24 percent increase, which looked to be about twice the rate of inflation.

The governor, using unusually strong language, criticized the SUNY system, calling its leaders irresponsible for not coming up with ways to limit budget growth. He went on to say, "The University was the only state agency that had failed to offer cost-containment ideas. They couldn't identify a single budget-cutting measure, not one penny's worth." A similar observation comes from a Capitol Hill staff member who recalls the summer of 1986, when budgetary hearings were conducted:

> **We saw the kind of expensive legal talent that some of the major universities had hired to lobby us; it suddenly dawned on us that we weren't just dealing with higher education in the nation's service. Rather, we were dealing with universities that looked and acted like the very large and very wealthy business corporations that they are. Suddenly, there was a consensus on the part of Hill staffers that these university representatives were**

well-heeled business people who were out after even more money. "Greed" seemed to us to be an appropriate term. We immediately resisted.

A retired professor from a large Midwestern public university who liked to keep comparisons – why I don't know – wrote that in 1988 his university had "TWENTY-FOUR vice presidents (counting in the associate and assistant vice presidents, but not the numerous assistants to the vice president)." The public university in the state next to his, of comparable scale, had 11. But, he reports, "The irony of the situation is that the one with more administrators has 12 faculty members in the National Academy of Science, while the one with fewer administrators has 43 faculty members in the National Academy of Science. ... The number of vice-presidents is at least inversely proportional to the number of members in the Academy."

A survey done by the private firm of Heidreck and Struggles, reported in the *Journal of Higher Education and National Affairs*, found that 46 percent of responding presidents believe the top-heavy bureaucracies of business and government are alive and flourishing in higher education. This survey was done in the late 1980s, yet the extravagant growth of nonteaching administrators continues unabated.

The retired professor who concluded the inverse proportion between numbers of administrators and numbers of faculty in the Academy of Sciences had this to say of his teaching load: "I was chairman of the department, and still taught 10 hours per week, but toward the end of my career it was reduced to six hours. The average load today [1988] at the university is 2.3 hours a week of undergraduate teaching." Under the code words "we must stay competitive," heavy bureaucracies get heavier, and teaching decreases. Our professor points out, "One year I taught more student-credit-hours than the School of Pharmacy, the School of Veterinary Medicine and the School of Mines combined, and these Schools had five deans, six secretaries, and some 20 faculty members." Our other professor, the one who went from 15 hours per semester of teaching to six hours and from writing eight books to none, concluded his letter with this commentary on the administration of the large public university from which he had just retired:

The proliferation of administration is laughable. And the problem of communication upward,

downward, laterally is a hopeless mess. It is easier to get the dean's attention by writing a letter to the campus newspaper than to him directly (and he has been known to answer in the same fashion).

There are such forthright and hard-working faculty members, some retired and some still active, just as there are some lean administrations. But there are too many bloated administrations, and they are not limited to the huge institutions; some small colleges feel the urge to build up the bureaucracy, often under the guise of providing better service, although often failing to so. A friend of mine called to ask advice about his son, who was having problems with his extracurricular activities. His son was attending a highly acknowledged, highly priced college. I suggested he call the dean of student affairs and have a good heart-to-heart talk. I warned him it might be tough to get to the dean, but I encouraged him to be persistent. About a week later he told me it took a while to get through to the assistant dean of student affairs, but he gave up when he couldn't get through to the associate dean of student affairs. As for the college, it had about 2,000 students, so it could hardly be considered a place in which to get lost.

But lost this student was, and the overgrown bureaucracy was not there to serve him. He transferred to another school.

Most people, including those inside our universities, do not realize the burden extra administrators put on the system. The burden is more than financial – it is demoralizing both to the faculty and the students. It develops into an unwieldy bureaucracy that is languidly impotent and often designed to ensure its continuance rather than provide leadership and support. It is no different from the bureaucracy of any large organization, whether in government or in industry. Whatever virtues being lean and fit once held, they are not in vogue now.

I had become president of a small to medium-sized college that had an unfilled position of vice president of the college. In 1988, creation of this position was strongly recommended by the Middle States Accrediting body, which is tantamount to a mandate. Using updated 2013 figures, the position called for a salary of $190,000. Fringe benefits of 24 percent increased the cost by $45,600. A person of this rank has his or her own secretary, which would come to $35,000 in salary and $8,400 in fringe benefits. Telephones, supplies, filing cabinets, computer, furniture, and anything else that goes into a top-level office was a one-time cost of about $15,000 and a continuing cost of about $9,000 annually. Next we computed the continuing cost of office space (heat, electricity, air conditioning). To this we added the travel costs for a vice president to attend one or two conferences. Not counting the $15,000 one-time cost, the total cost of the position came to $298,000 per year. It would take a 1¼ percent increase in tuition to fund this one position. And since the position would continue each year, so would the 1¼ percent increase. I decided not to fill the position, and in its place hired a part-time assistant who was already retired, sans secretary and sans all of the accouterments, for a yearly salary of about $14,000.

At one college with slightly fewer students than ours, but with a much longer history, it was observed that six full-time people were working in the development office: we had two. Their endowment stood at about $13 million, but so did ours. We had no capital indebtedness, and they did. We all ought to wonder about so many people being supported by a high tuition to achieve results that could be had for half the cost and with half the people. The excess number of administrators is a continuing burden that adds mightily to the cost of education. Service to the student and support for the academic programs are not enhanced by having extra administrators bumping into one another. What did Adam Smith say?

> **The discipline of colleges and universities is in general contrived, not for the benefit of the students, but for the interest, or more properly speaking, for the ease of the masters.**

Let me give an attention-grabbing example of how less administration is far better than more bureaucratic seeds. The initial incident was real and could have happened at almost any college in the country. A verbal altercation between two students at a party at a very expensive university, one male and the other female, soon escalated into a minor physical confrontation. I hasten to add that sexual harassment was not the allegation made by either party. Both parties brought charges against each other before the appropriate university committee, resulting in official reprimands to both, the male receiving a little more serious reprimand than the female. The outcome was protested vigorously by an on-campus women's group, who included a petition and a letter to the president accusing the administration of failing to support the woman. The president asked the provost to conduct an official administrative review, which he did in a 99-page report.

Whether by coincidence or as a result of the report, the women's group conducted a protest march, which prompted some male students to greet them with obscenities and moons. The dean called the situation intolerable, which it was, and went on to say that the problem is compounded by an erosion of student trust in the administration. Underlining the dean's point, the female student originally involved in the incident said that she wished she hadn't gone to the administration in the first place because it didn't solve anything and created a bigger problem for her. The women's group, whose march was greeted by loutish behavior, planned to avoid the administration and pursue criminal charges in court. The university planned to institute a large series of steps designed to prevent such occurrences, along with the hiring of yet another administrator to handle much of the new procedures. Whether or not this will work remains unclear either to the university or anyone else.

At just about the same period of time a female student came into my office with much the same story – a story that could, and does, happen on nearly any campus in the country. A party, verbal confrontation, and as with the university story, a very unclear picture of who was right and who was wrong. The more I talked with the student, the more I was convinced the incident was unfortunate and regrettable, but even Solomon could not adjudicate blame. To be more accurate, they were both to blame. I likened it to a basketball game where the intent is to play the game and not get into a tussle, but now and then a tussle occurs – not a mugging but a minor tussle. And more often than not, the referee warns both of them, or hits them both with a foul, or throws them both out. He realizes that to take testimony from the spectators would produce 99 pages of conflicting evidence, somewhat equally divided.

The young lady was appreciative of my time, my concern, and my comments, which included a suggestion that she and the young man either apologize to each other for their reciprocal uncivil behavior or, if they could not do that, then just avoid each other. They did avoid each other. There were no vice presidents, provosts, deans, associate deans, or a slew of others to make a mountain out of an incident that could be handled in a personal way in about a half-hour. Also, the results were more satisfying and truly more instructive than those produced by all the heavyweight bureaucracy that could be thrown into the fray.

I am not making a case that the president should get involved in all such situations. It could be a dean or an assistant. Indeed, our dean solved many a case satisfactorily to both parties without resort to larger administrations. In any case, common sense and appropriate good judgment must be exercised.

Incidentally, the women's protest march against the administration's action occurred during the April hosting program for prospective students and may well have turned off a few students and parents. These situations are a nightmare for the administration and extremely demoralizing for the admissions staff, who are responsible for recruiting the best and the brightest and then have their efforts greeted by what is the equivalent of a yellow journalistic headline that is in no sense indicative of the fine educational program at the university.

We ought to mention the simple, sympathetic, direct approach whereby the president or the dean handles the male/female controversy, ending in a solution acceptable to both parties is no longer possible. It has been 'outlawed' by a strongly worded regulation issued by the Department of Education in 2013. Henceforth, all colleges that receive any aid at all, whether given to the school or any student attending the school (which essentially means all schools), will be forced to assume the male is guilty, and he must prove himself innocent, in any matter between him and her that involves anything of a sexual allegation. This will include spoken words that she alleges are unwelcome. Just imagine the two of them coming back from virtually any movie, and he repeats what they just heard and she finds it unwelcome. It's off to the barricades for him.

What does this have to do with the high cost of attending college? Every college will have to develop a process to handle any and every complaint of a she said/he said nature. To do this, the college will have to load up on another office, more non-teaching staff, along with appeal processes and more people. The very government that laments the high cost of college is forcing colleges to spend even more. The University of North Carolina is one of the 20 or so colleges investigated for allegedly mishandling sexual-misconduct complaints. Their system has been a possible 20-step process with 'go-to' arrows everywhere. And it will get more complicated and costly. Consider that three students sued their respective colleges for denying them their due process. While the Department of Education's edict is going to be financially expensive for colleges to adhere to, it will certainly be used as an excuse for the many extraneous non-teaching staff on campus.

Business, industry, and government are often accused of mendacity. Believe us when we say, the infection of deception has struck the higher education system. Challenging our articles that colleges have too many non-teaching staff, Robert H. Atwell, a former president of the American Council on Education and a prominent lobbyist for more government spending on higher education, stated in 1987:

> **There is plenty of incentive for schools not to be administratively top-heavy. Private institutions are not making money. They are trying to survive.**

How any person in a position of prominence could make such egregious comments is hard to comprehend without assigning suspect motives. During the same period in 1987, then-Secretary of Education Bill Bennett stated that American colleges are rich, and their many Washington lobbyists are very good at getting money from Congress including loans for students, all of which encourages colleges to raise tuition. Twenty-five years later, there is almost universal agreement that this was an accurate forecast. Common sense dictates a connection between government largess to the buyer and higher prices from the seller. For me it began in 1974 when grants and loans were given to students based on the costs of the college. Higher cost: more aid from our government.

I was a dean at the time, listening to the VP for Administration explain a new concept. Raise the tuition a large amount, the government would provide additional aid, and following that the college would give a 'paper' scholarship to virtually every student which would give the students an even lower out-of-pocket expense. I'm sure other colleges used this ruse to get more government aid, until the government caught on to their ill-advised program and decided to give student aid after, not before all scholarships.

Once again Mr. Atwell, recklessly speaking for all the many colleges and universities that he represented, very bluntly said,

I would have expected the secretary – who to my knowledge is not a student of higher education finance, nor has he ever been responsible for setting college tuition – to have arranged for some careful analysis before speaking and writing on the topic.

Mr. Atwell, however, was president of Pitzer College in Claremont, California, and obviously considered himself proficient in setting college tuition. In 2012, Pitzer's cost for two semesters exceeded $50,000, and of course, the faculty have for many years enjoyed teaching three courses one semester and only two the other semester. Not much more needs to be said about having well-trained professional economists running our colleges.

College and university presidents often employ the three-step approach when tuition issues get hot. Step one is to carefully, and as earnestly as possible, acknowledge the problem. It is the time to "feel your problem." The next step, especially for those who head up public institutions, is to blame the government, at both the state and national level. The universal cry is "insufficient funding" – as if there ever was, or could be, enough tax support to feed this overweight and under-exercised body. The third step is to show true leadership potential by stating, somewhat equivocally, that this will be the last year for the large tuition increase, and that our problems will be solved and tuition increases will subside in the future. This is the smoke and mirrors in action. If there is a fourth step, it is hope: hope that the media will not revisit the subject, hope that parents will forget last year's statements, and hope that more than four decades of mendacity can continue.

In 2008, David J. Skorton, president of Cornell University, wrote an impressive article for the Nov. 21, 2008, edition of *The Chronicle of Higher Education*, titled "Higher Education: Special Interest or National Asset?" You will recall that the financial condition of the entire country was in trouble at this time. The article began, "The deepening financial crisis that is now affecting markets and people around the globe gives new context to what our nation is facing. Americans cannot think of business as usual in any sector of public or private life, including higher education." He goes on to list five things that higher education can do. The first deals with finances. "We must all work to aggressively and systematically reduce costs to gain savings, even if marginal, and use those savings to slow the rate of tuition increases. For our students and their families, every dollar counts." Before that comment, Cornell and most other institutions were averaging increases at twice the rate of inflation. In the five years since that statement, Cornell, and most other institutions continued unabated their previous track record of twice the CPI. Cornell in the 2013-14 school year now surpasses the $60,000 per year level.

***

There are two silver bullets that should be aimed directly at every high-cost college and university, private and public, and a third at Congress. The first is to be aimed at the scant teaching done by many of our faculty members and the second directly at the proliferation of administrators and other nonteaching staff. One can make a case that the former is the more egregious, and it probably is, but the latter, i.e., administrative bloat, has been consuming more of the high tuition increases lately. From a faculty point of view, it is setting a terrible example. How will we ever get faculty to understand that their privileged position must include a reasonable amount of teaching students if college administrations across the country are ballooning much faster than both student and faculty growth? In the work of Snyder and Galambos, written in the late 1980s, we read among their conclusions:

> **The cost of administering higher education has risen more rapidly than "educational and general" expenditures and more rapidly than "instructional" expenditures. Staffing data indicate a more rapid growth of nonteaching professionals (including administrators and other professionals) than of faculty.**

From 1989 to the present, nothing has subsided. Faculty teach less, non-teaching staff multiply. The faculty will be hard put to accept more teaching while the administrative ranks grow. To put it in the proper order, the number of non-teaching staff, at all levels, must be reduced if we are ever to get faculty to teach a respectable number of courses. Simply stated, the boards of trustees must question their presidents until the presidents dispense with the excuses and present realistic and sensible budgets.

What about Congress? Read on.

Chapter 4

Congress Enjoys Giving Away Money

Now for the third bullet, which should be aimed directly at Congress. On July 15, 1985, a hearing was scheduled by the Subcommittee on Postsecondary Education of the full Committee on Education and Labor, House of Representatives. The importance of the Committee hearing could not be overstated because it was an oversight hearing on the reauthorization of the Higher Education Act of 1965. This Act was the real beginning of substantial federal subsidies to colleges and students, other than aid that veterans received through the famous GI Bill. The Act of 1965 was revised in 1972, allowing just about all colleges to receive federal aid with no strings attached. Of course, some will say the piper always calls the tunes, and as we all have witnessed, a steady stream of regulations, whether for good or bad, have been issued out of Washington.

It is worth noting that not many years later, college prices began their unmanageable steep ascent to the mountaintop. Which begs the question: shouldn't the government largess have caused the price to drop? But then again, contradictions do exist; have we not seen that the colleges with the largest endowment are also the most costly? Of course, the real answer lies in the fact that reduced teaching loads began in earnest during this period; and also, coincidentally some would say, super large college administrations started their assent up the same mountain. This particular hearing in 1985 was to be held on the campus of Gettysburg College, headed by Chairman William D. Ford, Democrat from Michigan, and he was very upset. Just two months earlier I had written an article that was critical of the waste at so many colleges, and that waste included some of the government aid that helped jack up the price of college.

The article received wide coverage and also got Rep. Ford some strongly resentful constituent letters. The word I got sub rosa was that he was going to pin my ears back because I was causing him trouble – specifically, accusing him of wasting tax dollars. As expected, my testimony focused on the need for colleges to share the burden and not to continue the steep tuition increases. Rep. Ford questioned me closely about an example I gave the subcommittee. One of our students got a total just over $6,100 in all forms of federal and state assistance, but as a commuter, the total cost at that time was only $3,100. The student actually received $3,000 more in tax supported financial aid than he needed. After listening to the excuses from the representative, (after all, Rep. Ford implied, students need spending money too), it was easy to conclude that he, and many of the others, just wanted to give more tax dollars, costs be damned. Indeed, I received a copy of a letter Rep. Ford sent to another representative severely criticizing efforts to stop the wasteful spending.

It is contemporary wisdom that committees in Washington are pretty immune from direct accountability for the obvious reason that their fingers can point in many directions except inward. The following quotation taken from Rep. Ford's letter might assist in pointing in the right direction. "President Iosue implies that there is some relationship between increased federal spending for higher education and increased costs." He then went on to state that I was wrong. However, he did not mention that federal aid was given based in part on the price the college was charging. Higher tuition means more financial aid from Washington. Only someone totally immersed in Washington politics would believe that aid based on price would reduce the price.

He goes on to write: "However, college costs tend to lag a year or two behind general price increases, and the colleges are still catching up for the higher inflation rates of earlier years. One would predict that the rate of increase would come down substantially in the next few years." He did not say that he would predict it, but that "one" would, so finger-pointing could take yet another direction. What he may not have known, even though he fashioned himself an educational maven, was that reductions in teaching loads were all in vogue. Many colleges chose this general time period to reduce teaching classes for many professors, thereby guaranteeing huge and continuing tuition increases.

Also, I was alerted in advance that the Representative from Illinois, Charles A. Hayes, was going to pin me down on minority enrollment at my college, possibly creating an embarrassing situation. When he asked, "What percentage of the enrollment is minority?" I decided to play a little dumb, since I knew that he knew the answer: "I cannot tell you the percentage of minority students at my college, but I can tell you it is more than any other college at this table!" The discussion ended abruptly.

This was where I definitely learned that Congress wanted to give away money with no reciprocity from the colleges receiving the aid.

For the next two years, college tuition skyrocketed, so Congress decided to have another hearing, scheduled for Sept, 15, 1987. Chairman of the Subcommittee on Postsecondary Education was now Rep. Pat Williams, Democrat from Montana. He made it clear that he wanted no one from the Reagan administration to testify, nor did he want any dissenting views. However, the Department of Education, under the leadership of Secretary of Education William Bennett, insisted that members of Congress get a balanced view by having a member of the administration present, Chester Finn, assistant secretary for educational research improvement, U.S. Department of Education, along with my dissenting voice. As the hearing began on the morning of the Sept. 15, it was soon obvious that the speakers were stacked. Douglass Cater, formerly special assistant to President Lyndon Johnson, self-described "midwife" to many of the federal higher education financial aid programs, and president of Washington College in Maryland, was first to speak.

He was followed by William Bowen, an economist who was also president of Princeton. Then came C. Peter Magrath, president of the four-campus University of Missouri. These three gentlemen's testimony lasted into the early afternoon. Using up much of the time were the questions that were asked by members of the Committee. I was told the normal procedure was to hear all the testifiers, and following that then there could be questions. However, the Committee decided to spend excess time asking questions that reinforced the arguments made in favor of continued and increased financial aid. It was 3:20 p.m. when Chairman Williams said he was sorry, but there was a scheduled roll call vote, and the committee would have to leave in 10 minutes. He asked the fourth speaker, Edward Wilson, dean of graduate studies at Washington University in St Louis, to speak for five minutes, and I could finish out the last five minutes. Dean Wilson spoke for a little longer, which left me exactly two minutes.

Of course I was angry. The first three speakers had all the time they wanted, along with long, drawn-out answers to the many repetitive questions. More than this, all four speakers danced to the same tune ... more money. How much? More! And then some! Keep in mind, these were among the most expensive colleges in the country. And their endowments were very high. I was so angry that I blurted out, "Mr. Chairman, if I ran my college the way you run this committee, my tuition would be as high as these other colleges!" I got a few more civil words in, but not much. In reviewing what I thought were the minutes of the hearing, I noticed my comments were slightly reworded. It was my second lesson about congressional hearings. They are able to sanitize, to a small degree, the minutes before they are approved. And criticizing the chairman of a committee was not acceptable, even when warranted. But the bigger lesson was the total corroboration of the first hearing. They want to give out money, and lots of it. Is it any wonder that so few colleges have even begun to address their profligate ways?

The third hearing was quite different. The call came from the office of Rep. Patricia Schroeder, Democrat from Colorado. I had retired from the college, but was still active writing and speaking about the waste in higher education. She was chairwoman of the Select Committee on Children, Youth, and Families, and was going to hold a hearing titled "College Education: Paying More and Getting Less." Her interest was directed at the high costs, and she sensed that colleges were not doing much about it. She wanted to know if I would testify.

After my two previous hearings, I was not very interested, but I did say I would do it only if I had as much time as I needed. This was accepted and the hearing took place on Sept. 14, 1992. Dr. Richard M. Huber, a former academician who had just published a book titled *How Professors Play the Cat Guarding the Cream: Why We're Paying More and Getting Less in Higher Education*, joined me in testifying. Unfortunately, there were few members of the committee present, and while it was a well-run hearing, and even students from various high-cost colleges were allowed to testify about the high costs, the long-term benefits did not materialize. In Rep. Schroeder we had a powerful voice that could get things accomplished in Congress, but she decided shortly thereafter to leave Congress and work in the book industry. Tuitions everywhere continued their twice the CPI rise, even to the present day.

It would be easy, but wrong to conclude that partisan politics was at work: Democrats spend and Republicans don't. The last hearing showed a somewhat different agenda. They all enjoy spending, many of them more than others, and very few have the stomach to cut budgets or to even ask the tough questions.

A sizable portion of government largess is in the form of subsidized and unsubsidized loans. And here we must add that all colleges are willing co-conspirators. They politic and lobby for more loans, yet are not responsible if the student defaults on the loan. The sad ending is that the colleges' enrollments are increased with students who are under the obligation to pay back the loans decades into the future, as you shall now see.

It is safe to conclude the problem of high costs at colleges and universities started to ascend at roughly the same time the government decided to fund loans. For forty years the funding has increased, but at a lower rate than tuition has increased. At no time has the government assessed the value of its largess related to teaching audits or audits of non-teaching staff growth. One little example will tell much about their motives. Prior to the advent of online deposits, I spoke to some representatives to determine if checks issued by the government to students, requiring both the student signature and the college's signature, could instead be sent directly to the college for deposit into the student's account. The college would notify the student that the check was applied toward the student's tuition. This would save the college administrative time and effort getting students from everywhere to come in and sign and then deposit the check. It was in short, a labor saving device. Scamming or dishonesty was not involved. The representatives responding replied that their titles were on the checks, and that prospective voters needed to know this. As previously mentioned, this was not a democratic or republican issue, it was a political issue.

Reckless Loans Created a
Student Debt Bubble

Randy, a fine young student who often came into my office to ask advice, was wondering whether or not he should take out a Stafford Loan. These loans were formerly called GSLs (Guaranteed Student Loan), and they provided the student with interest-free money for college. The bank making the loan would receive the interest from the government until the student graduated and repaid the loan plus interest. The loans and interest are guaranteed by the government; there is no risk assumed by the lending bank if the student defaults. Randy qualified for the loan but didn't really need it because we had arranged some college aid and a part-time job, along with financial help from home. All in all, he could have done it tightly without the loan, but it was too hard to resist, so he took the government loan.

What I could not get across to him was that the day would soon come when repayment would be forthcoming. He might well think that on that fateful day he would be making a lot of money, but the facts are quite different, as you will see later on.

Colleges are motivated to help students get all the government aid and government-backed loans they can, because it eventually ends up in their coffers. Many needy students require help, but so many like Randy take the expedient and easy way, putting off any thoughts about loan payments down the road. As the vast majority of young college students know only too well, talking about paying back loans is as interesting and urgent as discussing their need down the road for long-term assisted living accommodations. Incidentally, many students are forced to pay back their loans over a longer period than first expected. Even the government sensed this and devised a program that allows the graduate to extend the loan repayment, often to absurd limits. In 2013, a young nurse explained that she got her loan payments extended to 25 years because, according to her reckoning, her salary would not support anything less. She was happy with the extended arrangement made possible by a compliant government, although she was virtually ignorant about interest rates and how much her loan would really cost her. Even if recent high school graduates are aware of some of the fine points of borrowing money, their minds are on the excitement and anticipation of entering college. They will sign virtually anything so they can begin this new and different endeavor. For the 18-year-old, 25 years down the road, rest homes, and cemetery plots don't compare with immediate adventures.

Does all of this financial aid pumped out by the federal and state (and in some cases city) governments cause the tuition to go up at unnecessary rates? Or, are costs of higher education independent of government support? We all seem to hold the view that government support of the health professions has caused everything connected with the medical field to increase, from prescriptions to operations to office visits. We all have the view that the billions of dollars spent on defense contracts and other implements of defense causes the price to go up. Why should higher education be any different? We have seen education become more and more like a regular self-interested industry that lobbies hard, markets even harder, and collects revenue like the largest of businesses. Is it just a coincidence that for about forty years, as government aid has increased dramatically, college costs have increased even more dramatically? When two events are so closely related, and so closely related directionally, the cause and effect become apparent.

One of the problems with government aid is that it uses the cost of the particular college in the formula that determines how much a student will get. The reason given is that it helps to allow poor people to attend expensive colleges. This may be well-intentioned but is unsuccessful, as shown in a study by a Harvard professor and a Stanford professor, and reported in The New York Times on March 17, 2013:

> **The findings underscore that elite public and private colleges, despite a stated desire to recruit an economically diverse group of students, have largely failed to do so.**

What it has succeeded in doing is providing more government money for a high-cost school than for a low-cost one. It is a policy that has a tendency to drive up tuition rather than lower it. No other government subsidy or support system works with this reverse psychology, i.e., if a person has more elegant and expensive tastes, the entitlement will parallel the cost. If Social Security worked that way, it would give a bigger monthly allotment to someone who bought a Cadillac rather than a Ford. Need-based Pell Grants, and other government aid that is based on need, frees up college endowment funds for students who do not need aid, but increases the prestige of the institution with their better academic training. Public institutions, as mentioned earlier, always were open to first generation students and those from low family incomes. However, in the senseless race for elite status, even they have focused more on higher income, better academically groomed students.

The end result of all this maneuvering is that the private elite institutions use their stature, their endowment, and the government largess to remain elite as they describe it. And many of the large public institutions violate their given purpose by limiting the needy in order to become part of the elites.

Another example that is often duplicated covers loans for graduate work. The years are the period 2009 through 2012. The three-year program had tuition and fees of $78,000. The student, Jeb, received a government backed loan of $123,355. The government, as it has done in the past, would say that the student needed extras to live on. However, totally private funds covered about $17,000 of the tuition, $57,000 for rent, $2,000 for books, and $13,000 for miscellaneous items such as medical insurance, car repairs, computer, and other items. The summary is staggering: $123,355 in loans, $89,000 in outside private funds, for a total of $212,000 to cover tuition costs of $78,000 and some extras.

There are two culprits working in tandem. The first is the giver of the money – the government. The second is the allocator – the college. It received most of the money, loans and grants made to the student, while remaining totally free of the obligation of the loan, even as the student is having serious problems making the payments.

Was the government ready and able to spend excessive amounts? Absolutely.

Were the loans easy picking? Yes.

Were the loans excessive? Yes.

Was the college financial aid office helpful in securing the loans? You bet!

Are the loans paid back? Some are; many are not.

Then, there are recent grads like Karen, who was obviously upset when she spoke to me about her student loan debt. The same story is heard countless times across the United States. "I racked up over $25 grand in loans getting a degree in mass communications," she said, "and here I am without a decent job, living at home. I can't really afford an apartment or a decent car until I land a good-paying job. I've sent out over 130 résumés and was only contacted once. Right now I'm working at a fast food place earning just above minimum wage, which at least helps me make my loan payments." Or consider Heather who found a good entry-level job at a fine hospital. However, her $25,000 student government loan had a payback schedule that was too steep for her salary. The government made an adjustment that reduced her monthly payment, but extended the loan to 25 years. When I discussed the situation with her, she was totally innocent about interest rates and, being very young, uncaring about the length of the loan. These are the very people who are expected to fund Social Security for older folks, pay off their student loans, and now have the added burden of mandatory health insurance to, once again, help cover the cost of older folks who are much more the users of health care.

There is no easy way out of this situation. Student loans are treated like a debt to the IRS. Even bankruptcy provides no shelter from these obligations. And, as you shall see, the total debt young people have been gratuitously offered is enormous and growing.

Not so long ago, a college degree was viewed as a strong academic credential that reflected well-honed job market skills. Lately, it has become synonymous with underemployment and crushing debt. According to the FinAid.org Student Loan Debt Clock, educational loan debt is growing at a pace of $2,853.88 per second. The following chart indicates that students, and in some cases their parents, now owe a larger amount of debt on their education loans than on their credit cards.

Student Loan Debt vs. Credit Card Debt

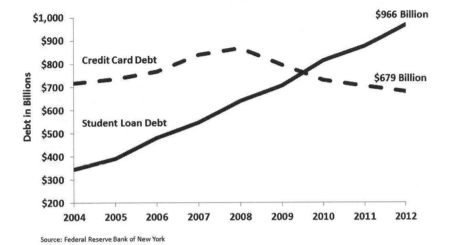

Source: Federal Reserve Bank of New York

The problem of the roughly $1 trillion in educational debt is exacerbated by the dismal job market prospects faced by graduates. A quarter of Rutgers graduates in a recent study were disappointed with their starting salary, with more than half reporting it was less than they had expected it to be. Likewise, a quarter had to work below their education level, and another quarter accepted a job outside their field in order to gain employment. Four in ten who graduated in 2009, 2010, and 2011 reported that they hadn't made any payments on their student loans. Making matters even worse, nearly half reported that they accumulated significant additional financial obligations such as credit card debts and car loans.

Unemployment for college graduates is well below the level for students with no more than a high school degree, but there are strong indications that many college grads are being forced to accept lower-paying positions that were once filled by those with only a high school diploma. According to a study conducted by Northeastern University researchers, more than half of recent graduates are jobless or underemployed, even in scientific and technical fields. The authors concluded that college graduates are more likely to work at Starbucks or a local restaurant than as engineers, scientists, or mathematicians.

By 2020, only three of thirty careers with the largest projected number of openings will require a bachelor's degree or higher: teachers, college professors, and accountants, according to The Bureau of Labor Statistics projections. The remainder are mostly lower-skilled positions such as home health aides and jobs in retail sales, fast food, and truck driving. The data also shows that as many as one-third of current college graduates are in jobs that historically have been filled by people with lesser educations. The U.S. now has 115,000 janitors with college degrees, along with 83,000 bartenders, 80,000 heavy-duty truck drivers, and 323,000 waiters and waitresses – a number exceeding that of uniformed U.S. Army personnel. Over the next decade, U.S. law schools will crank out four times more graduates than the projected number of open lawyer positions. The sad part about this last statistic is that all law schools know there is a shortage of jobs available, but they continue to promote their school to inquiring students.

The whole student debt scenario began when the Higher Education Act of 1965 was passed, establishing several grant and loan programs that made it easier for students to attend college. It was a noble and modest effort. More specifically, the Stafford Loan program was created, and interest rates were set by the government at a level intended to keep higher education costs within reach. The government guaranteed repayment of these loans to private lenders and still does.

When Uncle Sam opened the floodgates for subsidized loans without parent income restrictions to a wide range of college-aged students, higher education enrollments catapulted to unprecedented heights. Total full-time and part-time enrollment grew from 8.6 million to 22 million between 1970 and 2010. However, excessive loan debt figures also began to gradually run up and out of control when public money became too easy to acquire. And, as long as the price of tuition is in the government formula, our tendency will be to raise the tuition.

Our government should offer colleges much more benign neglect in place of aid that burnishes the golden college dome while the foundations of education at the K through sixth grade level develop

cracks, most especially at inner city locations.

As tuition prices continue to escalate, families are forced to pick up a larger portion of the tab. According to a Pew Research Center analysis depicted in the following chart, the average student loan balance increased from $23,349 in 2007 to $26,682 in 2010. More recently, student loan debt soared to $29,400 for the class of 2012, according to projections reported by the Institute for College Access and Success (TICAS).

Average Student Loan Debt (In 2011 Dollars)

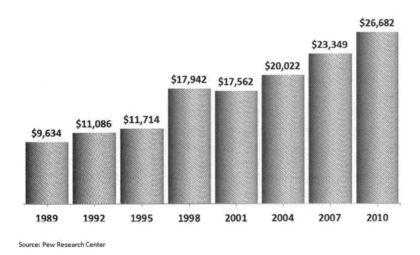

Source: Pew Research Center

Approximately two-thirds of the most recent college graduates have education loans. In 2007, 10 percent of student debtors owed more than $54,000. By 2010, 10 percent of student debtor households owed more than $62,000, with the highest concentration of debt centered in the Northeast. It is worth noting that most of the students in these graduating classes started college prior to the recent economic downturn, but the economy suffered a nosedive while they were attending classes. During that time, the chasm between rising college costs and the amount of financial support families could afford to offer, had widened dramatically.

In a typical business market, prices would be constrained by the disposable income of the consumers available to pay them. But easy-to-obtain government-subsidized loans circumvented all the usual barriers. College counselors encourage prospective students to accept loans as "a great investment in your future." Of course, these advisers are paid by the institutions that will benefit from the additional income. The graduates who were told that a diploma would open the door to success discovered that all it opened was the spare bedroom door in their parents' home, where they must now live in order to save money and try to pay off tens of thousands of dollars in debt. The sad part of this loan scenario is that banks, when making loans to almost anyone, home mortgages being a significant portion of those loans, have to provide all kinds of instructive literature to the person obtaining the loan. And if the loan is not paid back, the bank suffers the loss. But college loans are given to young incoming students, many of whom are totally naive newcomers to these sorts of long-term financial entanglements. And if student loans are not paid back, the tax payer suffers the most.

At the same time, colleges were given license to raise tuition prices and spend freely on extensive campus "trophy buildings" and expansion programs that would earn a few steps up the prestige ladder. "Higher education must make up for the mistakes it made in what I call the industry's 'lost decade,' from 1999 to 2009, insisted Jeff Selingo in a New York Times op-ed piece. "Those years saw a surge in students pursuing higher education, driven partly by the colleges, which advertised heavily and created enticing new academic programs, services, and fancy facilities. The almost insatiable demand for a college credential meant that schools could raise their prices and families and students would go to almost any end, including taking on huge amounts of debt, to pay the bill."

We will soon be recognizing the 40th year of continuing tuition increases that have risen, on average, at twice the rate of general inflation. An 8 percent per year increase means the cost of college doubles every nine years. Assuming the trend continues at that same pace, a baby born today will see college expenses three times higher than the current level when the child enrolls in college. "The cost of college rose 440 percent between 1982 and 2007, compared with the cost of living increases of 106 percent and family income growth of 147 percent," reported by John Leo in *The Newsweek/Daily Beast*. A recent poll conducted by *TIME* Magazine and the Carnegie Corporation found that "89 percent of U.S. adults and 96 percent of senior administrators at colleges and universities said higher education is in crisis, and nearly 4 in 10 in both groups considered the crisis to be 'severe.' "

During the past decade, families of college-bound students noticed that everyone else was taking on tremendous amounts of educational debt. Even knowing that the cost of a degree was rising into the stratosphere, they felt compelled to make the investment. Inexpensive credit loans helped offset the overwhelming price of college. However, when the dramatic economic downturn came along, home values dropped, jobs were lost, investments dropped, and those who were lucky enough to continue working found that their incomes were quickly losing ground against rapidly rising college costs.

The house of cards began to tumble when the number of high school graduates dropped and family incomes could not keep pace with soaring tuition rates, even with subsidized government loans. As a result, spending habits have drastically changed. Parents are struggling to maintain financial support for their children's college education. According to the Sallie Mae report on "How America Pays for College," students are paying a larger portion of their college bills (30 percent of the total bill, up from 24 percent four years ago), while parents are contributing less (37 percent of the bill, down from 45 percent). The percentage of families who eliminated college choices because of cost rose to the highest level since the study began five years ago.

Virtually all families exercised cost-savings measures, including living at home, adding a roommate, reducing spending by parents and students, and increasing student work hours. As a result, families parceled out 5 percent less for college expenses during academic year 2011–2012 than the previous year. Surprisingly, they also spend 11 percent less on private universities than they did four years ago. Parents decreased the amount they spend on higher education from their current salaries, savings, and investments. The overall theme from the research is that families and students are forced to be much more cost-sensitive regarding higher education decisions. Yet, the colleges still do not get the message.

In the past, college graduates were able to get a job, purchase a used car, and lease an apartment, which they may have shared with some friends. Now grads move back home with their parents, use public transportation, or borrow dad's car. An entire generation of graduates is being squeezed in an economic vise, and their primary focus is on managing education loans and credit card debt. It traps those interested in improving their standard of living by forcing them to work in low-paying jobs with mountains of debt. Being tethered to a voluminous loan limits the possibility of pursuing a long-term career at a lower-paying non-profit organization. Tighter household budgets have forced families to economize wherever possible on all expenses.

In light of the tremendous economic burdens that college graduates are facing, few were surprised when NBC cited "...recent U.S. Department of Education data which show the federal student loan default rate at its highest level in 14 years. The New York Federal Reserve recently reported more than five million student loan borrowers have at least one loan past due." The percentage of borrowers who defaulted on their federal student loans within two years of their first payment jumped to 9.1 percent in fiscal year 2011, up from 8.8 percent the previous year, and the total number of student loan defaults has doubled since 2005.

Economists are concerned about the escalating student loan defaults and their dire consequences on borrowers. Student debt is more toxic than a sinking mortgage because it is nearly impossible to walk away from an educational loan the way a homeowner can from a mortgage. Since student loans are not dischargeable in bankruptcy and are very difficult to have waived on the basis of hardship, borrowers are stuck. The IRS can seize income tax refunds until the defaulted loan is paid in full. The government can also garnish wages as a way to recover money owed on a defaulted student loan. Also, defaulting on a loan can adversely affect credit for many years, and a student who wishes to return to school cannot qualify for federal aid in the United States until satisfactory payment arrangements are made on the defaulted loan or the loan is rehabilitated, a process that can require as long as a full year of on-time payments.

Approximately one in every five of the nation's households has incurred student debt, according to the Pew Research Center. And the average loan in 2010, as we have seen, was nearly $27,000. The story has been repeated in other sectors of the economy. The purchasers believe what they're buying will increase in value and produce a strong return on their investment. The product grows more elaborate and expensive, but cheap credit provided by the sellers attracts more buyers. It all keeps going up until, like a Ponzi scheme, it collapses.

In addition to the high costs associated with undergraduate programs, graduate education charges have surged in recent years. As a result, a gargantuan increase in student borrowing has taken place at the advanced degree level, according to Jason Delisle, author of New America's report, "The Graduate Student Debt." The following chart indicates that the average amount of debt for students who earned a range of master's/professional degrees was $40,209 in 2004, $43,966 in 2008 and soared to $57,600 in 2012. These statistics are included in the average student loan debt figures depicted in the previous chart.

Median Student Debt for a Graduate Degree (in 2012 Dollars)

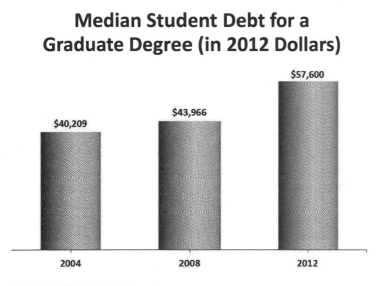

Source: The Graduate Student Debt Review

This trend is not restricted to the high-priced ticket programs such as law and medicine. For example, indebtedness for Master of Arts, Master of Science, and Master of Education degrees all followed a similar upward trajectory. The report goes on to describe "the alarming trends in what students are borrowing to finance graduate and professional degrees and, indirectly, what institutions of higher education are charging for those credentials."

Delisle is hopeful that the dramatic increase in borrowing for graduate and professional degrees will awaken legislators to the fact that there is no debt ceiling for students enrolled in these programs. Furthermore, since income-based government repayment plans provide loan forgiveness opportunities, it is unsettling to realize that many more graduate and professional students are likely to pursue that benefit in the coming years. A significant uptick in student loan forgiveness will place an even heavier burden on the government, and in turn taxpayers, since congressional legislation passed in 2005 allows graduate students to borrow an unlimited amount of money to attend school.

The upper 25% group of students who borrowed the most compared to their peers in 2004 is the same quartile that experienced the largest increase in 2012. That particular subcategory of graduate students amassed an additional $31,000 of debt – a staggering 57% increase in just eight years! As Delisle exclaims in the *Inside Higher Ed* article "Grad Student Debt Rising,"

> **That the extremes are getting more extreme suggests to me that things have gotten out of control.**

Knowing that graduate students, by definition, have already earned a bachelor's degree, one might assume that there would not be a tremendous amount of public funding available for them to pursue a higher level diploma. Yet, participants in graduate loan programs continue to reap an unsustainable loan bonanza. Is this the most appropriate use of taxpayers' dollars? Restrictions on these loan programs, including a limit on the amount of debt the government will forgive, is long overdue.

Just as we've seen at the undergraduate level, knowing students have easy access to loan money gives graduate schools license to raise tuition with no motivation for keeping costs down. There is little incentive to focus attention on the educational mission while eliminating outlandish amenities and bureaucratic waste.

The sad part in all of this is that young people are enticed by unscrupulous college counselors to borrow now to achieve the American Dream, and worry about the consequences later. But the high cost of an undergraduate or advanced education often doesn't play out well in purely economic terms. If too much money is spent, there is a human cost in deferred goals, reliance on one's parents for continued financial support, and a general lack of real self-sufficiency. Graduates become indentured servants, often working in compromising situations just to service their crippling debts.

During an alumni reunion, I ran into a former student, Todd, whom I've known since his undergraduate freshmen year. He proudly announced that he had gone on to earn his master's degree at a prestigious regional university. Todd came from a relatively poor economic background and had limited eligibility for academic scholarships. So, he was forced to borrow a significant amount of money to enroll in a graduate program, after already accumulating a sizable undergraduate debt. Todd's words still resonate in my head as he poignantly described his first-hand experience with student loans:

> **They say that the student loan program has made college more affordable, but that's not exactly true. Yes, loans make a college education more accessible, but that's a completely different concept. The reality is that when you finally walk across the stage with that diploma in hand, you still have to pay for it. And if you're saddled with a crushing loan obligation, you may be forced to delay or even forgo other important milestones in your life such as getting married, having children or buying a house.**

After so many fat years, colleges and universities have done little to improve productivity of instruction, learning outcomes and efficiency of administrative processes by embracing innovative cost-containment initiatives. Rising fees and increasing student debt, combined with diminished financial and educational returns, are undermining the notion that colleges are worth the colossal investment. Colleges must confront inefficiencies head-on to reduce costs and minimize barriers to achieving a meaningful educational experience for the students who are saddled with $1 trillion in loans.

It is a strange situation indeed where entering students, many of whom are relatively unschooled in the intricacies of loans, are helped and even encouraged by college financial offices to take out long term government-provided loans, while the loans end up in the college coffers, but the liability remains with the student. If the student defaults for any reason, the college remains in the clear while the student remains liable or in bankruptcy. Colleges can and should be involved in two aspects of this strange banking situation. They must offer sufficient instruction to every student who takes a student loan. Not just reams of paper stating terms and conditions. Colleges, of all places, understand that their incoming freshmen students have just recently reached the age of maturity; a time when signing anything is for the first time legally enforceable. They must understand interest rates, present value of money, compounding, and most of all, that the loan payment will begin whether or not they have a job, whether or not they buy a car on time, and whether or not they get married shortly after graduation. All of these situations do happen to many students, but as entering freshmen, understandably, they usually have other important things on their minds.

A novel idea would be to consider the following: everyone knows that seniors in high school, once they have been accepted into some college... whether two-year or four-year... breathe a sigh of relief. And for many, indeed, the overwhelming majority, there is a bit of "slacking off" on the normal class and study routine. For all seniors who will continue their education at college, mandate a crash course of a few hours a week for the remainder of the year that covers all pertinent aspects of financial loans. It will be an exciting change from the normal academic courses, and will help them understand what they are signing on to as they prepare to enter into the real 'adult' world.

The second issue that should involve colleges is concern over the numbers of loans it makes which end up in defaulted status. Some colleges have graduates who have low rates of default while others have high rates of default. Those that have high rates of default should be required to reimburse the government for a percentage of the loss if the default rate is an unjustifiable, repetitive issue.

Most Academic Scholarships
Are Nothing More than Discounts

I chuckled to myself when my neighbor proudly announced to me that his daughter, Kim, was awarded a $50,000 scholarship ($12,500/ year) at an area private college. I knew the young woman well and was aware that her high school grades and SAT scores were hovering in the lower average range. Kim participated in sports, although she was by no means an outstanding athlete. Her courses followed the typical college prep curriculum, although they were not heavy in the way of advanced level classes. She was certainly a good student, but by no means was she an outstanding scholar. I was also very familiar with the small Pennsylvania college Kim would be attending - a good school with fine programs and a tuition, fees, room and board 2012 cost of around $45,000 per year. I also knew that this college, like many others, was chucking truckloads of money into scholarships to attract enough students to fill their classrooms and residence halls. Little did my friend realize that the average new student attending that institution was receiving a reduction in price of $14,400/year.

There is an *Alice in Wonderland* scene going in colleges across this country. They gladly and prominently boast about meeting the 'need' of many of their students. What they will never tell loyal contributors to the college, and others, is that some of the aid is student loans, and all of the 'need' is created by the college itself, i.e. extraordinary high tuition and fees. As for the loans, they are a disaster in the making, as the previous chapter clearly showed. Many colleges have placed their tuition price (sticker price) so far beyond the reach of a large proportion of potential students that they feel forced to make up the difference between that price and what a student can, or is willing to pay, through institutional scholarships. This process of offsetting the sticker price with institutional scholarships for enrolling freshmen is known as tuition discounting.

Colleges tout their scholarship programs as a way to make their institution more affordable. In reality, it is a clever counterintuitive method for increasing revenue. That's right – awarding "merit" scholarships actually raises additional cash – but only if more students are enticed to enroll, and the institution has enough space to accommodate them. As described in Chapter 9, the number of high school graduates is actually decreasing, so not only is this approach failing, it is placing higher education in greater jeopardy by spending an inordinate amount of aid money on students who in many cases have minimal financial need or academic proficiency.

Rather than concentrating on containing costs and keeping tuition as affordable as possible, colleges have relied upon tuition discounting to achieve their bottom-line goals. In essence, tuition discounting has become the tug-of-war colleges and universities engage in to manipulate enrollment numbers in the hope of producing an acceptable level of income.

Simply stated, colleges have become much like car dealers by using a pricing pattern that charges different people different prices for the same product. Economists refer to this concept as "price discrimination." Colleges create varying price structures depending on availability of the product and how much the buyer is willing and able to pay. Cruise lines do this when they lower prices for those who buy near launch time, if quite a few berths are still empty. Airlines also use this technique to promote early purchases and, depending upon sales up to that time, last-minute transactions. Likewise, Broadway play tickets and hotel stays in Las Vegas can have huge swings in sticker price depending on when and where the purchases are made.

This is how it works. Let's say a college enrolls 1000 new students and charges $50,000 in annual tuition. That would translate into:

1000 students x $50,000 = $50,000,000 total net revenue

But, upon the advice of financial aid consultants using sophisticated analytical programs, the college realizes that if they offer a special group of 100 moderately higher-performing students a 25% discount, the college will gain an additional 50 students in that category. This strategy is known as "leveraging" financial aid to increase net tuition revenue. So, the resulting new revenue is:

900 students x $50,000 = $45,000,000
150 students x $37,000 ($50,000 – 25% discount)
= $5,625,000

Total net revenue = $45,000,000 + $5,625,000
= $50,625,000

The institution in this example gained $625,000 in net revenue plus any additional room and board income by offering a discount to slightly higher-achieving students. This works fine as long as there are enough additional students out there to attract, and sufficient space is available for them on campus.

Tuition discounting is calculated by dividing the total institutional grant aid by the total dollars received in tuition and fees. All money the institution awards to freshmen, including academic and athletic scholarships and grants of all types, are included in the formula. To keep the illustration simple, let's assume a college is charging $50,000 for annual tuition and fees. Let's further assume that 10 new freshmen are enrolling this year. Five have been awarded a $18,000 scholarship, five are receiving a $30,000 scholarship every year and no other college money has been awarded to these new students. The freshmen tuition discount rate would be as follows:

Gross Tuition/Fees revenue
10 students x $50,000 tuition and fees = $500,000
5 scholarships @ $18,000 = $90,000
5 scholarships @ $30,000 = $150,000
Total Aid = $90,000 + $150,000 = $240,000
Total Aid ($240,000) ÷ Total Revenue ($500,000)
= 48% FRESHMEN TUITION DISCOUNT

Using the car analogy, when sales are not where the auto manufacturer would like to see them, you will often see ads for rebates and low interest, easy-to-obtain financing. Sometimes these special prices are offered to first-time buyers or for purchases made during a specific low volume time period. Similarly, many institutions of higher learning would have empty seats in their classrooms and vacant rooms in their residence facilities if they did not discount generously. Conversely, if they lowered the sticker price enough to fill the empty seats and beds, their revenues might not be high enough to cover operating expenses. But, if they can attract some full-paying students while pulling in others with a lower price, they can at least fill their classroom seats and residence hall beds while securing enough revenue to operate adequately.

It is discouraging to note that very few institutions are promoting the notion that if colleges could operate with greater productivity and efficiency, costs would drop and revenue would increase. Of course, colleges do not relish the idea of being compared to car salesmen, so they develop an economic structure to complicate the discounts, with the ultimate result that has many believing their student actually received a prized and rare scholarship.

We'll double the price and give you a 30 percent discount!

"Poetic Deception" is the appropriate term. Talk to any parent whose child received a discount under the guise of a scholarship and you will notice the pride the parent takes in talking about the scholarship. Colleges willingly perpetuate the ruse.

Tuition discounting is little more than a glorified Ponzi scheme that seemed to work well during the early years, but became ineffective as colleges across the country raised their prices causing larger numbers of students to require increased aid packages while the tremendous growth in high school graduates came to an abrupt end. As public universities across the country are suffering deep budget cuts, an all-out war for additional sources of revenue, including the aggressive recruitment of out-of-state students, has ensued. Out-of-state tuition rates are often double the in-state price, so discounting those rates can generate increased enrollments and net revenue. So, even though very few people realize it, state universities joined in the tuition discounting game. The overall tuition discount rate at public institutions in 2007 was 18.3% according to a College Board study.

It's interesting to note that there are only a handful of financial aid consultants that colleges across the country use to configure their financial aid award packaging strategies. They all use similar statistical techniques called "econometric modeling," some a bit more sophisticated than others, examining historical enrollment data to predict how changes in aid will increase the number of students for the upcoming fall class. For example, if College A increases the discount by $1,000 to students from New Jersey who have a combined SAT score of 1100 or higher, that institution will likely attract 20 more of those students than last year. Furthermore, the net tuition revenue will increase by $150,000. So, even though the institution is spending more money in aid, it is getting back more operating cash.

That works out great, except the consultant then moves over to the competition, College B, who lost some of those students from New Jersey. You guessed it, after running the analysis, the competitor finds it necessary to increase its award to that same population, and so the vicious cycle continues. However, through all the sleight of hand, there are still many parents that are hit for the total undiscounted tuition. And the salt on the wound is that these full payers are not allowed to deduct part of their payment as a charitable gift.

As the following chart shows, the average discount rate at private, non-profit institutions reached a record high of 45% in 2012, according to the National Association of College and University Business Officers (NACUBO). This means that the average student at four-year independent colleges and universities received a 45% discount from the advertised tuition sticker price. The College Board data published in the "2012 Trends in College Pricing" indicates that only about one-third of full-time students and their families pay the full advertised tuition price without any institutional grant support, but the prices these students pay have been increasing dramatically.

Average Freshman Tuition Discount Rates

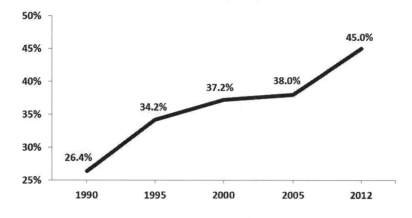

Source: National Association of College and University Business Officers

An amazing statistic revealed by the Institute for College Access and Success shows that even in 2005, four-year institutions awarded $3.3 billion in aid to students over and above their demonstrated financial need. In essence, the Ponzi discounting scheme is running out of steam as spiraling costs are so out of whack that students can't afford the heavy tuition costs even with steep rebates.

So, how did this insane discount game begin, and how did it get so out of hand? The phenomenon actually began in the early 1990's when the Justice Department Antitrust Investigation shut down the practice of elite institutions jointly reviewing financial aid offers of top performing students who were commonly admitted to the "Overlap Group" (Ivies plus MIT discussed earlier – categorized as a cartel). That decision is widely viewed as fueling the huge spike in merit-based awards that quickly followed.

Admittedly, some institutions discount their sticker prices not only to simply fill seats, but also to attract the brightest students, those with special capabilities, or to enhance geographic, ethnic or socioeconomic diversity. Others are absorbed in a competition to improve their prestige. They spend more dollars to recruit students with higher SAT scores and impressive high school academic performance credentials. Since those scores are frequently used to evaluate the comparative quality of colleges, enrolling more of them provides a greater chance to move up in the college rankings ladder, or improving the college's "profile" produced by *U.S. News & World Report* and similar guidebook publishers. Still, as tuition prices have far outpaced inflation over the past 20 years, college costs have reached levels that are shocking to the families of college-bound students and bewildering to virtually everyone else, including older folks who have benefitted from college in an era when all the various financial aid packages did not exist, but costs were reasonable.

So there you have it - colleges have turned to tuition discounting as a way to compensate for astronomical tuition rates which have accumulated after decades of rate increases well above the cost of inflation. But, that strategy has lost its effectiveness as the economic downturn has created a serious strain on family resources; fewer high school graduates are coming through the pipeline; government funding has diminished; and the financial need of families has surged upward. There is almost universal agreement that the current higher education high tuition/high discounting model is unsustainable and needs to change.

The time has long past for colleges to conduct business differently. Instead of playing a tuition discounting shell game to attract more students and revenue, perhaps it would be more prudent to roll up sleeves and pursue innovative ways of increasing efficiency and productivity on college campuses. At a few colleges efforts are underway to provide quality education to large numbers of students through various configurations of online education; collaboration with other campuses; streamlining administrative positions or reorganizing administrative units; and eliminating underperforming programs. There is a need to consider the outsourcing of appropriate campus services, faculty retirements and changing tenure policies.

Most importantly, we must seriously address the two humongous camels in our tent: insufficient teaching loads at so many of our high-priced institutions, including high-cost public colleges, and the vast growth of non-teaching staff that clogs our colleges and universities. Tough decisions need to be made to ensure that institutions are providing the highest quality education at the lowest possible cost.

For the millions of Americans who must rely on higher education to improve the prospects of achieving a fulfilling life, serious cost reductions in prices are critical.

College Charges Surge
as Graduates' Salaries Plummet

I was speaking with a father of two college students when he sighed and said: "You know, we spent way more money educating Tom and Jenny than we invested in our house. How is it possible for colleges to cost twice as much now as they did a decade ago, while a McDonald's hamburger went from 85 cents to a buck? Is a college diploma really worth twice as much now? Are graduates twice as smart?" Questioning the value of a college education is like questioning motherhood and apple pie. But with families suffering under the weight of oppressive debt burdens, household incomes declining or stagnating while higher education costs surge upward, and legions of graduates unable to find suitable employment, it's a fair and often asked question.

The unsettling fact is that the cost of a college degree has skyrocketed twelvefold over the past three decades. The following chart, based on Bureau of Labor Statistics data, shows that tuition and fees have soared past medical costs and way past the inflation rates for the Consumer Price Index.

Percentage Change in College Tuition vs Other Costs Since 1978

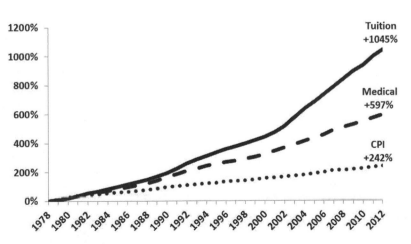

Source: Bureau of Labor Statistics

Over and above tuition prices, living away from home brings additional bills for housing, meals, books, all sorts of lab charges and other assorted fees, travel, and socializing. Just over the past decade, the cost of textbooks has tripled, and since 1982, room and board charges have doubled. It's not the colleges who are paying for these added expenses, but students and families, who are borrowing heavily, and I might add, are actively encouraged to do so by counselors at the institutions they attend.

The recent economic downturn and the inability of families to pay for astronomical tuition rates; growing pressure for governmental intervention to reduce costs; ever increasing levels of student loan debt; and the lack of good job prospects for graduates make it difficult for the trend to continue. Recent college-bound students have stated very clearly that their college choice was guided by price. In its National Annual Survey of Freshmen, the Higher Education Research Institute observed, "More first-year college students have concerns about their ability to finance college than at any time since 1971. Financial concerns also affected students' college choice, with 41.6 percent reporting that cost was a 'very important' factor in choosing which college to attend, the highest level since this question was added to the survey five years ago. John Pryor, survey director, says, "It's not about academic reputation. It's not about social reputation. It's about did you get aid at your first-choice college."

Students in the Pew study indicated they were more likely to place high importance on choosing a college where graduates land good jobs. The percentage of students reporting that getting a good job was "very important" increased to 56.5, the highest level since the question was introduced in 1983. *Time* reported that in the United States, 62 percent of jobs require a degree beyond high school; that share will rise to 75 percent by 2020. In 2010, "90 percent of college grads from 2008 to 2010 were employed, while only 64 percent of peers not attending college had jobs." A 2012 report on education and the workforce found similar results, with unemployment for recent college graduates at 8.9 percent, compared to 22.9 percent of job-seekers with just a high school education and 31.5 percent among high school dropouts. This appears to be a favorable report for college graduates until we read that many are in jobs that do not, nor never did, require a college degree.

College recruitment literature speaks about student loans as a higher form of investing in personal enhancement. Students are usually 17 to 18-years-old in their senior year of high school when they are told about college as an investment, along with the many loans available to them. Their knowledge about loans, interest rates, terms of payments, and investments is extremely limited, and their experience is non-existent. These 18-year-olds may be legal adults, but they have a lot more on their minds than legal matters. All they can do is hope that this "investment in yourself" will translate into enough income to pay off their massive amounts of accumulated educational loan debt when they graduate and get a decent paying job. However, more than half of all recent graduates are underemployed or in jobs that do not require a degree, according to an analysis of 2011 Current Population Survey data. The results showed that young college graduates were heavily represented in jobs that require a high school diploma or less, and were more likely to be employed as waiters, waitresses, bartenders, and food-service helpers than as engineers, physicists, chemists and mathematicians combined.

There were more grads working in office-related jobs such as receptionist or payroll clerk than in all computer/professional jobs. More were employed as cashiers, retail clerks, and customer representatives than engineers. In 1970, only 1 percent of taxi drivers were college graduates, but in 2010, 15 percent held degrees. The New York Times says, "Economists have referred to this phenomenon as 'degree inflation,' and it has been steadily infiltrating America's job market. Across industries and geographic areas, many other jobs that didn't used to require a diploma – positions like dental hygienists, cargo agents, clerks, and claims adjusters – are increasingly requiring one, according to Burning Glass, a company that analyzes job ads from more than 20,000 online sources, including major job boards and small-to-midsize employer sites."

The nation's colleges have simply turned out so many more graduates in recent years that their numbers have surpassed the volume of available jobs requiring higher level skills. In a report titled "Why Are Recent College Graduates Underemployed?" Richard Vedder said, "The number of college level jobs is growing at a slower pace than the number of college graduates, and it will continue to grow more slowly if government data proves to be true." In fact, Vedder and his co-authors project that over the next two decades, the number of college graduates is expected to grow at twice the pace of jobs requiring a bachelor's degree. Law schools produce more than 44,000 graduates each year, about two for every opening for a lawyer or judicial clerk, according to the U.S. Bureau of Labor Statistics. As reports circulate about unemployed graduates drowning in debt and suing their alma maters, the number of law school applications plummeted 25 percent in one year, according to the Law School Admission Council.

Subsequently, wages for recent graduates have fallen over the past decade, as depicted in the following chart. After significant gains in the 1980s and 1990s, salaries for America's young college graduates since 2000 have been steadily dropping. Because more people are graduating from college, it's easier for employers to insist upon degrees for jobs that previously didn't require them. Higher education provides a "credential" that employers use as a crude screening device to verify that the applicant is intelligent, conscientious, persistent, and generally knowledgeable – characteristics that may otherwise be difficult to evaluate. Employers are witnessing a glut of college graduates and are simply tacking on a degree requirement because they can. Furthermore, as manufacturers and business people use technology to reduce workforce costs during an economic downturn, they are finding that they can actually increase productivity – and profits – with fewer employees. In the past, this phenomenon occurred mostly at the expense of blue-collar jobs, but now it has cut into white-collar occupations. All of this has created a highly competitive job market.

College Graduates' Starting Salaries Have Fallen

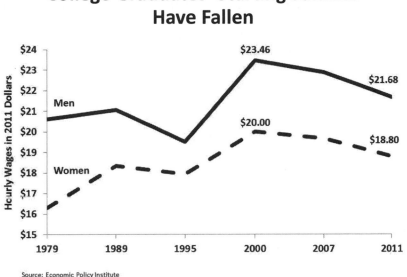

Source: Economic Policy Institute

The widening gap between what higher education charges and what families can afford to pay will continue to grow. Even community college enrollments have recently dropped across the nation following a period of huge enrollment increases since 2007. David Baime, senior vice president at the American Association of Community Colleges, said there was speculation that "people just couldn't afford it any more – even at these comparatively low-cost schools." States have cut funding on higher education by about 11 percent since 2010 to the lowest level since the 1980s. The Public Institute of California reported that as higher-education budget cuts have resulted in double-digit tuition increases, enrollment rates at UC and CSU have fallen by one-fifth over the past five years.

Many students are opting for overcrowded community colleges, and increasingly, high school graduates in California are less likely to enroll in any four-year college. The impact of states' funding, whether down or up has not produced substantive cost containment results. During lean years, salary increases are reduced, and during good years, it's "make up time". The sad fact is that tuition and fees continue their steep incline during both periods.

Although the number of students graduating from high schools has declined since the peak year of 2009, out-of-control costs and crippling student loan debt may be the real culprits. David Hawkins, director of public policy and research at the National Association for College Admission Counseling, summed it up this way: "I do think we've reached a tipping point in terms of what cost might do. The cost of college is really beginning to alarm families. And that creates a real threat to enrollment."

Unfortunately, most colleges and universities continue to function largely in a business-as-usual mode. Incredibly, in a 2011 survey, *The Chronicle of Higher Education* found that "a majority of college presidents believe that higher education is moving in the right direction. Almost four out of five (76 percent) say they are convinced that our higher-education system is doing a good or an excellent job of providing value for the money spent by students and their families." But then again, what would you expect a college president to say, especially one who is interested in staying employed?

As mentioned earlier, personnel costs constitute the lion's share of college and university operational expenditures. Bloated administrative staffs are expensive and stifle efficient decision-making processes. The antiquated tenure system, in effect, provides an amazing lifetime employment contract that no other occupation can dare offer — not exactly the best motivator for innovation and productivity. *Money Magazine* ranks college professor as the second-most desirable job in America, under software engineer, based on several factors, including an average annual salary of $81,491. Those annual pay averages have been known to exceed $200,000 at some top-tier universities. On top of that, between 1988 and 2004, faculty teaching loads dropped by 42 percent at research institutions and 32 percent at private liberal arts colleges.

Another desirable aspect of being a professor is that there are no mandatory standards for staying up-to-date. All other professionals: doctors, dentists, engineers, lawyers, etc., have certification requirements as the years roll by. Even cultural professionals have their various audiences to consider, whether actor or musician. This is not a call for mandatory standards to be implemented for all tenured faculty members. Rather, for them to realize they are taking advantage of the plum they are now enjoying.

The financial impact of this systematic reduction in workload on the operating budgets of colleges across the land has been dramatic, and the trend needs to be reversed. Of course, that is not taking into account fall break, Thanksgiving break, a month to six weeks off for the holiday season, spring break, Easter break, and an entire summer without any required work! Even when school is in session, not many hours are spent in the classroom. Working conditions tend to be cozy and cordial, with minimal travel demands. Unlike high school students, college students typically select their courses and are more motivated to attend. Is it any wonder that a university professor is the least stressful career according to a 2013 CareerCast "Jobs Rated Report"?

Another reason universities have become so expensive is because they feel compelled to offer a full complement of peripheral services, somewhat like a small city. It is not unusual for campuses to operate hospitals, entertainment operations, hotels, catering services, etc., when these might be outsourced to more efficient specialists in those respective areas. The lavish building wars and massive subsidies for athletic programs are way overdone and need to be ratcheted back to contain spiraling costs. Programs that are not pulling their own weight should be reduced or eliminated as inappropriate rather than continuing the practice of simply adding new items to the list.

Facilities on our nation's campuses are notoriously underutilized. Schools should explore the possibility of leasing space during off times. Colleges could avoid some unnecessary construction costs by collaborating with other organizations to share common physical plant resources whenever appropriate. Institutions should band together to increase their bargaining power with various vendors.

As chapter 11 describes in greater detail, the spread of high-speed internet access, wireless technology, smartphones, tablet devices, Facebook, and the cloud has supercharged online connectivity in just a few short years. A generation of students has grown up on these new technologies and is much more comfortable learning and interacting with professors through these mediums. Schools such as M.I.T., Stanford, Harvard, Yale, and a rapidly increasing number of other universities have invested tens of millions of dollars each to offer lectures through free massive open online courses (MOOCS) which are readily available to anyone. Potential income-producing strategies include agreements with publishers that are seeking to sell their products to the droves of students who register for MOOCs; employee-recruiting services who want to reach the best students; licensing of courses to other universities; and charging students a fee to enroll.

Unfortunately, faculty at some schools, feeling threatened, have already began mounting an offensive against any such move. Their claim, while somewhat valid, is that students need the in-class teaching and experience. The obvious contradiction is that faculty have fought for years to have reductions in teaching. We must also remember that the 1970s was when TV was expected to become education's savior. "Sunrise Semester" was developed as a model to show the world that TV education could reach millions who could not attend or afford classes. Even then, faculty feared the handwriting on the wall, and happily helped its demise.

Colleges should help students save money by providing accelerated study options, such as three-year degree programs, to more efficiently move students through the bachelor's degree process. Another opportunity is the dual enrollment model, which allows high school students to enroll in college-level courses that will be applied toward a degree upon matriculating at the sponsoring institution. Textbook expenses can also be reduced by encouraging the use of electronic versions of books as well as rentals. The days when students were advised to hold on to their textbooks for a lifetime is over for most texts.

Our four-year colleges, public and private, including those that have been marginally classified as universities, along with our historic universities ... all of them can learn a thing or two from our two-year community colleges. Being ranked is of minor or no interest, having overly elaborate buildings does not really impact education. Getting out of classroom teaching is not even a tertiary concern – quite the contrary, classroom teaching is a primary concern. Lean administrations are an asset. Self-service is not an overwhelming consideration in making academic decisions. In a nutshell, two-year community colleges have managed to remain true to their laudable mission. Most of our higher-level institutions have not. Regrettably, the situation has become debilitating for college graduates who find themselves saddled with enormous debt coupled with reduced earning potential to pay their obligations.

My Campus is Bigger than Yours
– The Edifice Complex

In my former position as Dean of Student Affairs, I was always intrigued by our Food Services Committee meetings. Typically, some food service managers, a group of students, a faculty member and one or two representatives from the student life area were included. Student initiated conversations frequently started out along these lines: "We visited a nearby small private college and discovered that they offer more extended meal hours, serving food until 2 a.m. They also provide a greater variety of meal selections that include a steak entrée five days every week. We also noticed that they have a Burger King, Pizza Hut, and Starbucks right in the Student Center. Why can't we offer those kinds of things on our campus?"

My usual response was: "Those special amenities can be expensive. Who would pay for the additional expense?" The inevitable answer: "The college should pay for those services just as they do at the other institutions." I can't help but smile inside when I think that these were the same students who complained about tuition increases, even as we received national acclaim for keeping tuition increases below the CPI. Students are always seeking additional services and amenities and colleges are often too quick to accommodate them with little regard to the financial consequences.

We were also looking to replace or upgrade an aging gymnasium facility that was fraught with structural limitations. A team of faculty and administrators was formed to research the latest configurations on other campuses. The recommendations that resulted from the information compiled during the investigation were stunning. It was not at all unusual for even smaller colleges to have recently constructed lavish sport and fitness centers with features such as multiple gymnasiums - each surrounded by 4-lane running tracks, field houses, several indoor tennis and racquetball courts, three specialized fitness rooms, each equipped with state-of-the-art cardio and weight-training accessories – one for students, another for sports teams and a third for alumni and guests, climbing walls, a 20-lane Olympic-sized pool with multi-level diving boards, water slides and lazy rivers, multiple dance and exercise studios, golf simulators, bowling alleys, a collection of personal trainers, extensive locker room facilities, well-appointed lounges with large flat screen televisions, skylights, outside patio cafés, food court areas, a host of conference rooms, as well as plush administrative, sports and recreation management offices.

When asked if all of these accoutrements were really necessary, responses from the Physical Education faculty and coaching staff seemed to focus on three basic themes: "We must go for first-class if we want to be the best." Or "we have the opportunity to create a prestigious 'wow factor'." And "we need to stay competitive to attract the most outstanding students."

> **The assumption here is that the more the institution builds and expands in a quest to excel, the more it will prosper. If not approached in a strategic, mission-critical fashion, the exact opposite can easily occur.**

Whenever a consultant rides onto campus to offer guidance on virtually any extensive project, one of the first questions posed is: "Can you provide me with a list of aspirant colleges - those higher level institutions you would like to emulate?" That has become the name of the game. Every institution has its sights on moving up the food chain, becoming bigger and better known. Some community colleges focus on four-year institutions. Small, lesser-known private schools envy the second-tier elite colleges, or replace the moniker 'college' with the name 'university'. And, of course, the second tier elite institutions pursue the Ivy League universities. The Ivies battle among themselves to achieve top dog status. A glance at any strategic, long range plan for any institution in the higher education community will quickly validate the commonly known perception that colleges and universities are trying to be Rolls-Royces and no one wants to be a Chevy or a Toyota. Simply put, they refuse to acknowledge that their student bodies are not all above average.

In fact, it is not unusual for students of modest means to feel out of place when surrounded by the luxurious accommodations of many campus environments. But, the reality is that the Malibu or the Camry can easily, comfortably, and less expensively get you where you want go.

The chairmen of our Board of Trustees asked us "How come we are such a successful college?" Without thinking too much, the immediate answer was: "The good Lord made more average and slightly-above-average college students, and we acknowledge that fact and stick to that mission."

The "bigger and more ostentatious is better" mindset has helped fuel the explosion of construction projects, expanded auxiliary programming, and bloated administrative bureaucracies on college campuses throughout the nation. The baby boom echo enrollment surge that occurred during the past decade proved to be the catalyst that launched massive fundraising and building campaigns. Based on data collected by College Planning & Management magazine, the chart below traces the meteoric rise in higher education construction spending.

Total College Construction Costs

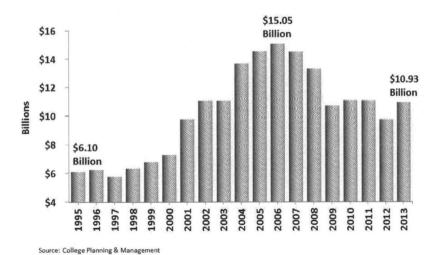

Source: College Planning & Management

Since tracking began in 1995, the five year period through 1999 remained relatively stable at between $6-$7 billion. Beginning in the year 2000, total college construction exceeded the $7 billion level and shifted into high gear. During the succeeding two years, it reached $11 billion. By 2004, colleges and universities construction rose above $11 billion, peaking at $15 billion in 2006.

As one would expect, the effects of the recession, including decreased gift giving and tightened credit markets, have impeded growth in this segment of the economy. In 2009, construction dropped to $10.7 billion and remained around that level through 2013 when it reached $10.9 billion ($7.5 billion in new construction, $2.0 billion in additions, and $1.4 billion in renovations).

Over the past two decades, construction and real estate development on college campuses experienced a higher increase than any other industry except health care, in both the number of projects and the dollar amount per project. Basically since 1994, higher education construction headed in an upward trajectory, doubling in volume, in sharp contrast to residential and commercial building project expenditures which suffered a modest decline. Frank and Cook describe the nonproductive competition to expand facilities and upgrade campus amenities in higher education as an "arms race." In a message to *The New York Times*, Richard R. Vedder, director of the Center for College Affordability and Productivity, said that "the Edifice Complex pervading higher education flies in the face of other trends that call for caution in capital spending."

Institutions of higher education claim they need to build fancier dormitories, dining halls, student centers, and gymnasiums to attract students. Since 1981, room and board rates have jumped an average of 5.3% every year, and dorm rates are rising faster than apartment rentals in general. A study conducted by the Bureau of Economic Research confirms that many four-year colleges do indeed invest heavily in student life amenities to recruit the majority of students who are unable to enroll in highly competitive institutions. Upon reviewing the data, it appears that all students appreciate "consumption" items which include student services, activities, athletics, student health, residence life, and related facilities.

However, the researchers disturbingly concluded that only those students who attend highly competitive institutions value academic spending enough to influence their enrollment decisions, whereas the vast majority of college-bound students will not be swayed by spending on academics. In an *Inside Higher Ed* article, Jane V. Wellman, founder of the Delta Project on Postsecondary Costs, Productivity and Accountability, stated that "it's the second-tier institutions that throw money at the consumer side of things, hoping to hang onto students and to move up in the rankings. They can't compete with the big dogs, and have found that students with money are willing to spend it on things that have immediate and tangible benefit."

> **More proof that the Chivas Regal Effect is alive and well on college campuses.**

It is no surprise that the United States system of postsecondary education spent nearly $30,000 per student in 2008, more than twice the world average ($13,461), according to the U.S. Department of Education. Expenditures per student ranged from $5,780 in Estonia to $20,903 in Canada, $21,648 in Switzerland, and $29,910 in the United States. The U.S. spent 2.7 percent of its GDP on higher education, which was well above the average percentage spent by other countries (1.5 percent), and higher than any other country reporting data.

Colleges and universities frequently indicate that cutting capital spending would undercut prestige, which relates to securing adequate enrollments and successful fundraising. The concept of academic quality, general reputation, and prestige is often correlated with guidebook rankings exemplified by *U.S. News & World Report*. Ironically, these ranking do not compute job placement after graduation or average starting salaries by major. They don't even assess specific academic learning outcomes. Rather, they measure such factors as the amount of money spent on student life programs and services per student. Using those kinds of criteria means the more expensive, less efficient schools are always the best ones.

In an attempt to develop more meaningful consumer information, some newer college rankings, such as the Forbes/Center for College Affordability and Productivity (CCAP) survey, use various web-based data sources including the PayScale Salary Survey of salaries and MyPlan. com's online statistics regarding how satisfied students and alumni are with their overall college experience. However, even surveys using this approach suffer serious credibility issues. This particular ranking is limited in scope (610 schools), as a very large number of schools have no available data on the variables measured. The statistics that are used also may be questionable in terms of applicability and bias. More importantly, none of the surveys measure what students knew when they entered, in relation to what they learned when they graduated.

Sam Dillon, reporting for *The New York Times* on the results of a study conducted by the Delta Cost Project, a watchdog of college costs, summarized the findings: "American colleges are spending a declining share of their budgets on instruction and more on administration and recreational facilities for students... . The trend toward increased spending on nonacademic areas prevailed across the higher education spectrum, with public and private, elite and community colleges increasing expenditures more for student services than for instruction."

Examples of questionable expenditures are not difficult to find:

Penn State decided to construct new classroom buildings so students could avoid scheduling unpopular morning classes, even though the University's Strategic Plan indicated the facilities were underutilized.

The University of California system contracted for $8.9 billion in construction projects at its 10 campuses while cutting billions of dollars from the operating budgets of its public universities because of declining enrollments.

A California University of Pennsylvania report noted that a market analysis prior to the construction of a new convocation center recommended that the arena should be about half of its ultimate size, and caused construction costs to grow by $6.2 million due to design changes and errors.

The University of Chicago's Cultural Policy Center investigated cultural building projects in the United States and found that 80% ran over budget, some by as much as 200%.

Workers renovated a theater complex, installing new seating, lighting fixtures and a high performance sound system at Valley College in Los Angeles. But, even before the $3.4-million job was completed, officials decided to construct a new theater complex. The renovated one is slated for demolition.

At L.A. City College, architects designed a five-story fitness center with a glassed-in dance studio on the top floor. Before construction began, the college decided to move the fitness center to another location on campus where a shorter building profile was required. The original $1.8-million design was suddenly worthless and the architects were paid $1.9 million to draft a new one.

Florida State University announced a five-year, $75-million state-supported plan to move up from its listing as number 42 into the top 25 public universities in the *U.S. News & World Report* rankings.

New buildings are also springing up on campuses because donors have a strong desire to be immortalized. As one college president explained to me: "donors don't get excited about dorm renovations or scholarships because they aren't as visible as a shiny new sexy building with their name attached to the front of it." The same is true of the presidents themselves. A legacy of bricks and mortar, with a specific building displaying the president's name, is a long-term monument not all that dissimilar to the pyramids of the pharaohs.

But, these capital projects have dire budgetary implications beyond the initial construction costs. Institutions frequently borrow heavily on vast expenditures, and interest payments on bonds are often paid out of operational budgets funded by tuition. Between 2002 and 2011, total debt at public four-year colleges more than tripled to $88 million according to the Department of Education. Then there are the additional maintenance and repair costs, additional equipment expenses, outlays for utilities, etc., that also need to be taken into account. Inevitably there are extra custodial, security, building management, and other support costs associated with such projects, all affecting tuition. Here is an example of how expenditures for facilities have become exacerbated by the extravagant costs of extraneous employees.

It was a warm and pleasant day when a number of us parents went to watch the Parents' Weekend football game; the stands were about half empty. What we saw was two middle-level teams compete while we had fun with our kids, enjoyed the afternoon sun, and forgot the score by dinner time. What I could not forget was the enormous staff that accompanied the main coach onto the field. Out chugged assistant coaches, backfield coaches, line coaches, equipment managers, trainers, and a few other former jocks whose exact role I could not figure out nor, I doubt could anyone else. This was not major league stuff, this was not the powerhouses from Division I that we see on television or hear about week after week. This was not one of the very few colleges whose football team actually makes money for the athletic program. This was fun and games, enjoyable division II stuff, yet modeled after the few big-time programs that actually make money.

In this regard, there is a similarity between athletics and research, even though these two aspects of college life cannot be more different. The similarity is in approach, in attitude, and in institutional state of mind. In research we have a relatively few of our full-time faculty members capable of and actually producing research of such high quality as to deserve released time from teaching. Yet thousands upon thousands of faculty members are teaching less than they should on the erroneous premise that they are or should be doing very seminal research. What is good and deserving for the few is extended to countless others, and we have seen how this unjustifiably raises the cost of education. In athletics, relatively few of the 3,600 colleges and universities that field athletic teams actually show a profit, yet hundreds upon hundreds of others create athletic staffs that copy the big boys, all because if it is good for the big boys, it must be good for us.

There are basically three divisions in the NCAA (National Collegiate Athletic Association): Division1A or so called Bowl Division and 1AA so called Championship Division (about 120 teams in all depending on the various intensity of sport, e.g. only basketball for Georgetown) consists of the heavyweights that supposedly make money for the institution. But those accountants who can get their arms around the variety of ways of keeping the financial accounts say those that actually make money are few; no more than 20 of them bring into the college more than they spend for football. The vast majority of small to medium-sized colleges are in Division III, where no money is made, scholarship are forbidden, and there is a lot of pure fun in the games. Division II is in between, meaning it does not make money, some scholarships are allowed, and virtually all Division II colleges try to copy the big guys in Division I.

As I watched a Division II team play a basketball game against our

Division III team, I knew that one team had a part-time coach while the other had four coaches sitting on the bench each repeating the instructions of the person who evidently was the head coach. The score of the game was a one-point difference; the outcome of the coaching was one dedicated part-time coach easily overmatching a small fleet of supernumeraries. What really piqued my interest was a conversation I struck up with a gentleman who was making notes feverishly while watching the game. It turned out he was a spotter for yet another college that would soon be playing one of these teams. I asked him if he volunteered his services or was paid by the college. He was being paid. The big boys have paid spotters; why shouldn't the little guys have the same? But the copycat mentality we have seen with research is flourishing with athletics and, once again, it jacks up the cost unnecessarily.

In the business world, officials keep a sharp eye on the bottom line, minimizing the costs and related upkeep which erodes profits. New construction always must be justified in terms of return on investment. But in higher education, cost containment is on the back burner. For example, a prudently and reasonably built dormitory will actually show a surplus of income, even after all expenses are taken into account. This will help hold tuition for all students to a lower level. An athletic center, as previously described, will send the cost right through the roof and require a significant tuition increase, even if the center is paid for by donations. Operating costs can be extravagant, and usually are paid with increased tuition. Professor Bob Gurland of New York University described it picturesquely:

> **If someone wants to give you an elephant, just remember it eats a lot, and there is a lot of cleanup afterwards.**

When the proper perspective is in place, cost savings solutions can often be achieved in a simple, straightforward manner. Lander Medlin, Executive Vice President of the National Association of Administrators, says "Universities use their existing academic buildings about 40% of the time. The optimum time for faculty and staff for classes is 10a.m. to 2p.m., or maybe let's give it 9a.m. to 3p.m., and that's Tuesday, Wednesday and Thursday." A report from the California's Legislative Analyst's Office reinforces that perception by recommending that campuses should make more efficient use of academic building space by scheduling more morning, evening, weekend, and summer classes. There is this common joke among administrators that you could shoot a cannon down the hallway of virtually any classroom building in the United States on a Friday afternoon and no one would hear it.

I was involved in a medium-sized private college that, like many others, was enjoying a spike in enrollment during the mid-1990s. The near future projections clearly indicated continued strong growth in the student body and since classroom space had become very tight, faculty were clamoring for a new academic building. After reviewing all the options, we devised a plan that would shave a few minutes from every class period and extend the semester by approximately one more week. This new configuration provided the exact same number of classroom hours per semester. But, it also created an extra time period every day in every building. In effect, it created the space of a new building without the added expense and upkeep of a construction project. In came some negative reactions from professors with comments that their traditional vacation time was ruined and they were now forced to work an additional week without pay. It is worth noting that the faculty are paid an annual salary, not a weekly one.

It is typical for colleges to add new programs and structures without considering cuts in existing, unproductive or obsolete programs – they find it easy to add, but difficult to subtract. Each new program receives additional resources, and institutions rarely examine budgets with the idea of allocating funding on the basis of mission-critical priorities. Intercollegiate athletics in particular is almost always not self-supporting, yet, according to Robert Dickeson, in a report issued to the Commission on the Future of Higher Education, receives a disproportionate amount of internal financial support, which simply adds to college costs. Across Division I schools, athletic department spending was 3-to-6 times higher than the average overall amount institutions spent educating students, according to a recent study conducted by the Delta Cost Project.

Operational efficiencies must be established to control unnecessary expenses. Collaborations with other institutions to share library services, some academic and student activity programs and certain administrative functions such as mail delivery, maintenance, human resources, and group discount purchasing opportunities are options worth considering. A reallocation of resources to critical educational programs and support services, and effective hybrid models of learning delivery systems can improve retention and graduation rates while lowering costs for students. These, and other efficiencies, should be considered by all colleges, but we must be vigilant that they are not used as straw men for the main culprits: bloated administrations and reduced teaching.

It's painfully clear that boards of trustees and presidents need to collectively hit the brakes on eye-popping construction projects that have overleveraged colleges and have played a role in pushing tuition prices beyond the reach of many who must rely on the higher educational system to provide a pathway to a more fulfilling life. Leaders must also put a halt to the unbridled expansion of support and administrative costs. Every campus needs to focus on strategic mission-critical goals that help define what is appropriate to invest in and what should be avoided in order to begin the process of making college costs reasonable again.

A Future with Fewer Students
and Lower Family Incomes

A stunning revolution is shaking higher education in the United States to its core. Demographic change is happening in a lightning quick pace and dramatic fashion, according to recently released projections by the Western Interstate Commission on Higher Education. First, colleges and universities have enjoyed more than 20 years of uninterrupted enrollment growth, especially throughout the past decade as children of the baby boomers, known as the baby boom echo, graduated from high school. During that period, colleges responded with unprecedented building expansion projects that in many cases included luxury residence halls with single bedrooms, private baths, the latest technological conveniences, and a wide variety of gourmet meal choices. It was not unusual for a campus to showcase an opulent new student center with tons of large-screen televisions, skylights, and atrium; or a dazzling athletic facility equipped with bountiful state-of-the-art fitness equipment, climbing walls, and other recreational amenities.

From 1998 to 2008, national college enrollments grew from 14.8 million to 18.6 million students, an increase of 26 percent, surpassed by a dramatic surge in spending on student services, according to the Delta Cost Project study. Richard Vedder, director of the Center for College Affordability and Productivity, summed up his impression in a statement to *The New York Times*: "This is the country-clubization of the American university. A lot of it is for great athletic centers and spectacular student union buildings. In the zeal to get students, they are going after them on the basis of recreational amenities." The following chart projects the number of high school graduates beyond the high-water mark of 3.4 million students (adding up the indicated totals for all four regions) in 2011.

> **The accelerated college enrollment growth
> has come to a screeching halt.**

This has caused the admissions people at all colleges to stretch their efforts. Not just the front- line staff who actually cover the beat, go out to high schools, meet with families, and walk the talk. The VPs and deans of enrollment management who devise the plans, do the statistics, who used to be well-versed and confident in ratios of applications received compared to enrollees, are now trying new systems, and are very unsure of what to expect. The new enrollment environment for all schools is dramatically different, and more difficult. This new environment, while uncertain for many schools, may be helpful in forcing them to more fully work with budgetary matters and enrollment in a complementary system, as opposed to relying solely on enrollments to fulfill budgetary expectations.

Projected Change in High School Graduates by Region, 2011-2028

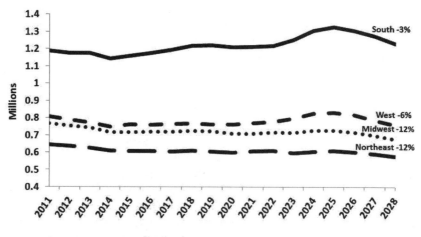

Source: Western Interstate Commission for Higher Education

The shrinking of the national supply of high school graduates began with the class of 2012, and it will continue to decline until stabilizing from 2014 through 2020. After that, the graduating classes between 2021 and 2028 will experience very modest growth that will still fall short of the 2011 peak figure. For the Northeast and Midwest, the scenario is even more daunting. Those regions will see a general decline in high school graduates throughout the entire projection period ending with the 2027–28 academic year. In effect, these areas will experience an average 1 percent drop in high school graduates each year, although there will be some mild fluctuation bumps throughout that period.

Colleges in these areas will find themselves in shrinking markets and facing intense pressure to fend off more aggressive competitors while expanding or altering their own recruitment strategies as they seek to attract students from new market areas themselves. Many private schools will continue to get caught up in the tuition discounting bidding wars, providing more and more financial aid to students to offset their higher prices, in the hope of enticing more enrollees, a trend that many view as unsustainable. Others will accept a decreased enrollment posture by eliminating expensive, underutilized programs with the goal of trying to establish a higher-quality, more elite institution.

Another alternative is to simply downsize administrative structures and programs to cope with fewer classes and reduced revenue. Some institutions will sacrifice admission standards and enroll students who are less academically prepared than the current classes the colleges are serving. Another strategy is to target efforts at attracting older adults, international students, and other nontraditional populations. Still others will pursue innovative approaches to establish more productive classroom learning delivery systems, including various configurations of online instruction solutions.

We have heard several seasoned college presidents comment: "Oh, back in the '60s they were predicting a drop in high school graduates that would create a devastating blow to higher education enrollments, but that never happened." Well, that's sort of true. Although the number of high school students did decline, according to the National Center for Educational Statistics, the percentage of those students who enrolled in college jumped from 38 percent in 1960 to 51 percent in 1975. Then, from 1975 through 2010, the college enrollment rate gradually increased from 51 percent to a record high of 70 percent. The effects of a sluggish economy and the widening gap in salaries between high school and college graduates have accelerated the trend.

The significantly declining number of high school graduates masks the fact that more students of color than ever before will enter the nation's colleges in the coming decade. The following chart illustrates that minority students will account for 45 percent of all high school graduates by the year 2020. As the white population declines, Hispanic and Asian/Pacific Islander numbers will flourish nearly everywhere.

Projected 30-Year Change in Composition of U.S. Public High School Graduates by Race/Ethnicity

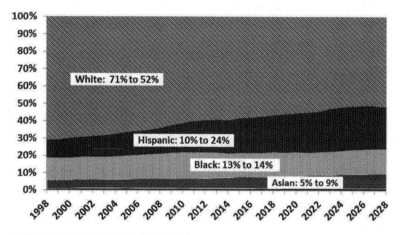

Source: Western Interstate Commission for Higher Education

In the coming decade, the number of white high school graduates will decline 12 percent, blacks will drop 9 percent, Hispanics will climb 41 percent, and Asian/Pacific Islanders will increase by 30 percent. Hispanics for the first time became the largest minority group in 2011, comprising 16.5 percent of all students attending the nation's four-year colleges and universities, as reported by The Pew Research Center.

There are measurable differences in college enrollment rates by racial backgrounds. The National Center for Education Statistics (NCES) reported that in 2010, the percentage of high school graduates who entered a two or four-year college the following fall was 88 percent for Asians, 70 percent for whites, 66 percent for blacks, and 60 percent for Hispanics. Between 1990 and 2010, high school dropout rates also declined for whites (from 9 percent to 5 percent), blacks (from 13 percent to 8 percent), and Hispanics (from 32 percent to 15 percent), while Asians/Pacific Islanders remained at 4%.

Unfortunately, the nation's track record at the postsecondary level in serving underrepresented populations has been consistently lacking, and the need to improve is critical, since the economic and social consequences are potentially drastic. The NCES data shows that the six-year college graduation rate is 69 percent for Asians, 62 percent for whites, 50 percent for Hispanics, and 39 percent for blacks.

A college graduate strolling through campus after a 20-year absence will notice a markedly different composition of the student body. The growing minority population has affected all aspects of campus life, including the variety of ethnic meals that are being served in the dining areas, the cultural themes of campus activities, and the scope of advising and counseling services. William Frey, a leading analyst at the Brookings Institution, was quoted in USA WEEKEND Magazine about the rapid change that is taking place across the country: "Hispanics really are a very big part of America's present and future. And they're not clustered in one area. They've been fanning out to all parts of the United States, and by moving into new parts of the country ... they're becoming accepted by these communities."

Nowhere has this influence become more apparent than in the 2012 presidential election, when Republican candidate Mitt Romney captured a huge majority of votes from the white population, but lost his bid for the nation's highest office. President Obama won re-election by amassing 80 percent of the Hispanic, black and Asian ballots. Mr. Frey summed up the phenomenon: "The role of minority groups, especially Hispanics, has frankly, shocked a lot of people when they looked at the result of this election. People thought this was going to happen 20 years from now."

The financial implications on the higher education community are also affected by the lower income levels of the new generation of students who will be entering their campuses. The latest U.S. Census Bureau data indicates that the average Hispanic family household income in 2009 was 34 percent less than that of non-Hispanic whites, while African-Americans' incomes were 36 percent lower. The implications of the changing composition of the new generation of students for colleges and universities are far-reaching. For starters, the attainment gaps of underrepresented students must be addressed to improve learning outcomes, retention levels, and graduation rates.

The bottom line is that not every institution may survive the coming years. The opportunities for securing consistent sources of income are constricting at an unsettling pace. "Economic, demographic, marketplace, and technological trends are converging to cause an unprecedented time of change for higher education. The new reality is that colleges are expecting to have to do more with less for years to come," according to Tony Pals, spokesman for the National Association of Independent Colleges and Universities. In an interview with *The Wall Street Journal*, Laurie Joyner, president of Wittenberg University, Ohio, emphasized that "if colleges do not adapt to shifting demographics and the weak economy making families more price-sensitive, there will be fewer institutions." Declining demographics, dwindling productivity, weak revenue streams, staggering tuition costs, and stiff economic headwinds make it ever more critical for those in the higher education community to face up to their stark inefficiencies.

As competition for students heats up, and as the search for additional sources of revenue continues to intensify, an even higher proportion of students requiring significant financial assistance in order to attend is a haunting prospect. Clearly, fewer and fewer families will be able or willing to dole out lofty tuition payments in the future. Furthermore, any additional recruitment outreach activities and support services to accommodate these students will exact a financial toll if not approached from a strategic vantage point. Colleges and universities need to examine their operations, make some tough decisions, and abandon the wasteful practices that have lunged costs well beyond a reasonable level for the American families who must rely on higher education to pursue the opportunity for a more fulfilling life.

Self-Interest with Hubris

Whether in business or in education, it is important to market our product or service. In order for colleges to obtain more revenue, questionable practices are sometimes used. For example, there has been a recent surge in higher education institutions that have rebranded themselves as universities, often in an effort to raise their profiles and attract new pools of prospective students. "The associations that people make with colleges are very different from associations they make with a university," said Elizabeth Scarborough, chief executive of Simpson Scarborough, a higher-education market research firm in Alexandria, VA., in an article titled "University Is the Name of Choice for Many Colleges." "When people think of a college, they think of a small institution with a bucolic campus. When they think of a university, they think big – tons of resources, lots of majors, expansive facilities, very strong research programs, and long lists of graduate programs. The connotations are so strong that colleges tend to be less appealing to prospective students than universities." James Owston, dean at Mountain State University, refers to the phenomenon as "peer pressure." Schools and colleges "feel left behind if they're not universities." Yet these new names, in many cases, don't match the college's reality.

This pernicious form of self-aggrandizement is very costly even though it appears to have no extra costs attached, because it is not as visible as a shiny new expensive athletic hippodrome. The traditional description of a university as opposed to a college has been hijacked. Formerly, a university had a college at its center, and then there would be schools surrounding it, for example: a school of engineering, school of education, school of business, law school, teaching hospital, and possibly others. Virtually every state in the Union has a landmark state university with a school of agriculture as provided by the Morrill Act. Universities would be large and varied, offering advanced degrees such as doctoral degrees and even some post-doctoral work. They also would specialize in many forms of research. Because of this, their teaching load might be expected to be lower than at places where research was at the scholarship level.

The American Association of University Professors, along with other organizations, records annual salaries by institution and professorial rank. This is done so that all institutions can know what other institutions are doing regarding salaries and fringe benefits. In general, university professors make more than four-year college professors, including those colleges that offer master's degrees. However, and this is the catch, if a college changes its classification to a university, then the erroneous presumption of research is made, along with the clear expectation that salaries must match those of legitimate universities, and worst of all, in-class teaching must be reduced. Colleges across the country caught the bug and petitioned their respective state departments of education to reclassify them as universities. They were all obliged, with no effective standard used in the process. It became both a fad and the rage. Small colleges, medium-sized colleges and virtually all state colleges (formerly state teachers colleges) applied for and were granted the new classification. The extra costs to both student and government would soon follow – and will continue for the foreseeable future.

Consider SAT scores, a test used by a vast number of our schools as one criterion for determining admission into the college. The ACT is the other big player in testing for admission to college. The higher the score, the better the chance of a student getting into the school of choice. And even though some institutions downplay the role of the SAT in deciding whether or not to admit the student, we are all impressed by the higher SAT. Can college after college have average SATs higher than the national norm? We expect a basketball team to be taller than the average person, but it would be fanciful to read that everyone in the general population is taller than average. Some colleges have found a way around the dilemma of having students with SATs lower than they wish to be. They just don't count the students at the bottom of the list. All of us in education knew these colleges played little games with SATs in order to have a higher average than really existed, because they wanted to look better and more selective, to be able to raise their tuition even higher. How was it done? The most common way was to admit the lower-SAT students as probationary or require them to take a remedial course; put them in a summer program first; or put them on a waiting list and then admit them after the SAT computations are made. Any device was acceptable, as long as a special category is created for students with lower SATs. How bad had the situation gotten? The College Board agency wrote to all directors of admissions in 1988:

It appears that some colleges have been reporting [SAT] figures for the entire freshman class, while others have been excluding some or all of their "special admits," that is, students who for some reason do not fit the normal academic profile.

We always want to put our best foot forward – that is understandable – but what the College Board is talking about, and what many of us on the inside knew, was that liberties of such magnitude were being taken, all in the name of marketing, as to distort the admission profile and reap benefits from higher tuition. The warning from the College Board included creative reporting methods being used with the ACT scores, rank in class, and high school grade-point averages. One of the reasons for this questionable maneuvering was to elevate the college's reputation within the "best of" lists such as US News & World Report's annual assessment journal. These lists are very attractive to people unaware of their intrinsic shortcomings. More recent reporting standards require colleges to include scores for all entering full-time freshmen, including summer students.

However, a February 1, 2012, *Chronicle of Higher Education* article titled "Inflated SAT Scores Reveals Elasticity of Admission Data" reported: "The same numbers to which applicants and parents – not to mention presidents and trustees – often attribute great power and meaning, are, like most things on the planet, subject to manipulation. For better or worse, the admissions industry operates on an honor system that governs the flow of 'self-reported' data submitted to the federal government, accreditors, bond-rating agencies, and publications such as *US News & World Report*. The common data set has standardized the information colleges provide to various outlets, but admissions officers say interpretations of even the most basic information vary from campus to campus." Duplicity redux.

A gentleman wrote about the frustration he has encountered with his alma mater, a very high-priced, upscale college that would not listen to his pleas to hold tuition down. The only answer he continually received to his entreaties was: "It cheapens the image." A president, now retired, of another similarly high-priced college said the tuition was going up 9 percent that particular year, and the primary reason was because the other 10 colleges with which his college floated around was doing the same. It is well-known that many colleges operate together in small cohorts, such as the Ivy League, consisting of eight colleges, or Amherst, Williams, and Wesleyan.

> **Are they cohorts or
> are they cartels?**

Ursinus College, a fine relatively small college in Pennsylvania, brought in a consulting firm some years ago to assist with marketing strategies that would lift its image within its peer group of colleges. One of their recommendations was that a significant tuition increase would price the college near the top of its peer group and would succeed in dramatically raising perceptions of quality.

In a more radical viewpoint, consultants recommended that Washington University in Missouri could increase its already significant academic reputation, without much change in academic programs, if it raised its tuition one dollar more than the highest-priced college in the land. While these events happened years ago, the perception is healthy and alive today, and the paradoxes abound. There are few marketing advantages tied to lower tuition. Even if the college is financially healthy, the high tuition is regarded as a sign of excellence. So pervasive is this practice that it is often referred to as the Cartel Effect. All schools that run in a pack practice it, more knowingly than unknowingly. Combine this with the Chivas Regal branding, and the result is a strange policy that runs counter to the great American free enterprise strategy that if competition thrives, the quality should improve and the price decline.

The Mount Holyoke story is a perfect example of an outstanding college that practiced cost-containment under one president and, over a period of time, felt it was losing out to its peer competitors. Under a new president it charged all the market could bear, spent a lot of this additional money on many things unrelated to education, and soon felt its position was more competitive. Part Chivas Regal and part cartel. The Chivas Regal Effect is having the label on display, while the Cartel Effect is to work in conjunction with your competitors. It reminds me of the story of a legislator who was still harboring a grudge at Bucknell University because it rejected his daughter. She went to a "lesser" college, he told me.

"Where is she now?" "Well, she graduated and is now in graduate school at Yale University." "Where would she be if she had been admitted to her first choice?" He thought for a moment, not so much because he needed time to find the answer, but because the question forced him for the first time to realize that the Chevy got his daughter where she wanted to go, as would have the Mercedes. He also realized he saved quite a bit of money in the process of his daughter getting to her goal.

The Cartel Effect is an interesting phenomenon and may run counter to the law, as mentioned earlier on with the Ivy League. In the early 1990s, the Justice Department in Washington charged the eight Ivy League colleges, along with MIT, with being a certifiable cartel, a serious charge that the schools resisted. Even though the schools were located in different "cost of living" environments, their prices were very much the same and their tuition increases were very similar over the years, as were their scholarships. Their admissions people met with each other to discuss acceptance of students. All of this, and more, came out during investigation. They got a cease-and-desist order from the Justice Department, which the Ivies accepted while MIT protested, but to an outside observer, not much has changed over the years.

David Breneman, then president of Kalamazoo College, was quite open in an article he wrote for *Change Magazine*, in which he pointed out that no college within its peer group wants to deviate dramatically from the pricing patterns within its group. He went on to say that a reasonable budget may call for a 6 percent increase, but when we learn that our peer group is at 7 percent or 8 percent, we have little choice but to match it. The 2 percent excess may not seem much, but compounding over the years has got us into the fix we are in now. The process is tantamount to price fixing. Phone calls are made, information exchanged — all the elements that would get the car business or the paper business or any other business in trouble with antitrust laws. The philanthropic nature of higher education provides some protection.

Some states have enacted laws forbidding its public institutions to increase tuition beyond a given percentage. Obviously the legislators feel the colleges in question are unable or unwilling to act responsibly with tuition increases. How do these colleges react? They introduce new fees or dramatically increase existing fees that are separate from tuition. As an example, consider the state of Massachusetts, which limited the increases allowed for its public colleges. Salem State University is pretty similar to all the others. It has a very low tuition of $910 for the year 2013–14. But it has a "university fee" of $7,540, which is more than seven times larger than the tuition. Among its other fees, it has a $40 resident hall fee and a dining hall fee that ranges from $75 to $255. These are not room and board costs, they are extras.

Or consider the University of New Hampshire. For 2013–14, its tuition is $13,670. But you must add $965 to that if you major in engineering or computer science. Or add $946 if you major in business, and $800 if your major is music. Of course they have other mandatory fees that apply to all students. They are:

Student Activity $102

Health and Counseling $589

Student Union $359

Student Recreation $492

Student Athletics $983

Technology Fee $182

Transportation $119

For a total of $2,826

These are examples, but nearly all colleges, public or private, have fees that are not usually reported when the media announce large tuition increases. As a rule of thumb, you can often count on fees that may exceed 10 percent of the listed tuition. Some rather strange fees found at other colleges are an "enrollment fee" and a "capital projects fee." What are they? Who knows? Deception aplenty! It is often said that sometimes excellent students will later on surpass their teacher. If banks are superb in teaching us how to add fees to everything we do, then colleges have been excellent students in surpassing the banks with its list of fees.

Where does the extra money go? Since there are endless demands for expenditures on campus – some good, some not so good – all the money will all be spent. We will manage to spend every penny we get, even if it is more than we need. As far back as 1980, the well-known and respected educational economist and then-president of Princeton, William Bowen, wrote in his book, *The Costs of Higher Education*:

> **Each institution raises all the money it can, each institution spends all it raises, the end result is toward ever-increasing expenditures.**

As previously pointed out, institutions with some of the largest endowments also have the most expensive sticker price. But here again, it should be mentioned that endowments are categorized by size, and being near the top of the list is a measure of significance and is not in any sense related to the listed price of attendance. Who was it that described the nature of endowments so succinctly?

> **An endowment is like a pond that always wants to grow to be a lake.**

Technology Can Be a Wonderful Servant or a Dangerous Master

Books will soon be obsolete in the schools...our school system will be completely changed in the next ten years.

While it can be safely stated that technological advances can surely have a dramatic impact on our lives in the long run, short-term predictions frequently fail to align with reality. A good case is point is the above quote from Saettler's *History of Instructional Technology* which cites Thomas Edison in 1922, predicting the revolutionary impact of motion pictures in American classrooms.

In 2013, the average amount of money spent on information technology was $925 per every full-time equivalent student – that's close to $1 million for every 1,000 students - or 4.4% of the typical college's budget, according to the EDUCAUSE Center for Analysis and Research. Mary Stephens, vice president of finance and administration at California State University, expressed her perspective on technology budgets:

As everyone in higher education is aware, technology spending can constantly increase and still not seem like enough.

And that is the real danger of technology – it can easily turn into a black hole, unnecessarily consuming gobs of money, often just to quash the fear of falling behind in the prestige race. Having the latest bells and whistles garners lots of favorable press coverage. Those huge, interactive, multi-touch, multi-use video walls, and plush video conferencing centers look really impressive during the all-important campus visit tours. And a friendly help desk with overflowing numbers of support staff assures mom and dad that their student will receive all the support required to thrive in a college environment.

That is not to say that technology does not have a great deal of warranted merit. We all realize that nearly every aspect of our lives has been touched and improved in many ways through the development of innovative technologies. Examples include robotic medical surgery procedures, safer automobiles, healthier foods and ergonomically designed seats. The same holds true for higher education.

Through the years, the notion that an innovative technological advancement would revolutionize the entire education experience has frequently emerged. Just about every new invention has been touted as a big game-changer for schools. Education consulting organizations vigorously promoted programmable typewriters, educational televisions, microfiche, motion pictures, film projectors, VCRs, CDs, and DVDs. More recently, the same applies to desktop computers, laptops, tablets, mobile phones, and other wireless smart devices.

Because mobile devices have become powerful little computers in their own right, college students can easily access a plethora of digital resources and services including eBooks, course syllabi, class homework assignments, shuttle bus routes featuring real-time vehicle locations, online classes and registration timetables, as well as calendars for social, academic, and athletic activities. Through Near-Field Communication (NFC) and cloud storages, students can wirelessly exchange documents, audio and video files, photos and other images with professors, and submit homework assignments.

Students can download from vast libraries of videos, music selections, and podcasts. Another benefit of smart devices is the ability to conveniently contact classmates and professors from nearly any location at any time, perhaps through a social network application or simply via emails, enabling the user to access help to review and discuss assignments. On many campuses, directions to various offices, personnel photos, and faculty advising hours are available at the touch of a few buttons.

Now that Voice over Internet Protocol (VoIP) has arrived on the scene, video conferencing is available between multiple smartphone users. Students can remotely interact with one another to complete team projects without meeting at a physical location. An entire class can virtually attend a lecture or meeting with the use of VoIP-enabled equipment.

Professors have also adopted the latest computer devices and software programs to efficiently plan class presentations, assign grades, communicate with students, and perform other classroom tasks. Many have creatively and seamlessly integrated new technologies and social media communications into their classrooms to enhance the student learning process.

On the administrative side of things, technology can offer some notable cost-saving efficiencies. Online self-service programs for course scheduling, for example, provide students with 24-hour access to register for classes and pay their tuition bills, while assuring the monitoring administrators that classrooms are being filled expeditiously. On the other hand, it is easy to be lulled into purchasing software programs and features that sound attractive when presented by a motivated vendor, but ultimately turn out to be frivolous, as well as financially untenable. A campus-wide digital imaging system may seem like a great idea. A paperless office, with easy access to electronic files for all employees, must be a good thing, right? For some large universities that option may make sense and actually reduce expenses. For smaller institutions, an initial investment well over $650,000 with an annual maintenance fee of $55,000 may be overkill. In that instance, perhaps the installation of a more modest and inexpensive stand-alone version which can be effectively shared by key employees in two or three essential offices, would be more appropriate.

A strategic, data-driven approach to technology purchase decisions is more critical now than ever for institutions to operate efficiently in pursuit of their mission-critical goals. Can virtualization (dividing one physical server into multiple environments with software) provide savings on small, independent web servers? Is it necessary to replace fax or copying machines that can be incorporated into a nearby printer, or centrally managed? Can desk-side printing devices be replaced with fewer cost-effective regional printers that are shared by multiple users? Should lab computer screens be replaced every four years instead of three? Will enhanced training increase performance and efficiency, reduce attrition and raise customer satisfaction?

Joining a higher education technology consortium offers reduced pricing and peer collaboration, accompanied with the additional benefit of sharing valuable information and strategic resources. Oftentimes, perfectly acceptable free or low-cost products are made available to colleges, such as Google's email service, Apple's iTunes U, or YouTube

EDU. In some instances, it may make more sense for institutions to leverage economies of scale with outsourcing, or appropriately reconfigure current staff responsibilities, as opposed to purchasing expensive computerized systems that require costly periodic updates and additional support staff. But that overall attitude is lost on many college administrations that pride themselves on acquiring the latest high-tech accoutrements on campus at the expense of students' hard-earned tuition dollars.

Another significant cost-savings measure is the judicious employment of student interns who are engaged in related science, engineering and business majors to work side-by-side with the information technology professional staff. This not only provides supplementary assistance for the department, but offers valuable hands-on experience in their field of study while it provides some welcome extra cash for the student.

When viewed from a creative vantage point, technology can offer unique solutions to challenging issues. At the University of Maryland, students protested the ever-rising costs of textbooks, according to a recent article in *University Business*. "Students wrote on a whiteboard explaining the costs of their textbooks, some claiming they paid over one hundred dollars for one book while another student paid nearly a thousand dollars for a semester of books." University officials took the messages to heart and initiated a pilot program to transition all required course materials to online open source textbooks. Since open source textbooks are not protected by copyright restrictions, anyone with Internet access may use the materials at no charge. When fully implemented, the project is expected to save around $160,000 for 1,100 students. Unresolved issues inherent in that undertaking revolve around the identification of appropriate materials needed by professors to compile new textbooks, and the development of manageable quality control mechanisms. The report indicated that similar programs were initiated at Massachusetts Institute of Technology, California State University, and Washington State College.

Technology does have some drawbacks. In a study reported in *The Chronicle of Higher Education*, Oppenheimer and Mueller provided students with laptops or pen and paper to take notes in their normal classes. Subsequently, students were tested on how well they recalled facts and applied concepts. The researchers discovered that laptop users tend to take verbatim notes, which has become an increasingly popular technique, resulting in reduced understanding of content compared to those that selectively used hand-written notes. Mounting research and evidence on technology initiatives indicates that hardware and software, in and of themselves, result in no increased academic achievement. Steve Jobs, co-founder, chairman, and CEO of Apple Inc., in a 1996 interview with *Wired*, explained his position on the subject:

> **I used to think that technology could help education. I've probably spearheaded giving away more computer equipment to schools than anybody else on the planet. But I've had to come to the inevitable conclusion that the problem is not one that technology can hope to solve. What's wrong with education cannot be fixed with technology. No amount of technology will make a dent.**

Others see things quite differently, especially in regard to higher education's hottest and most controversial topic – Massive Open Online Courses (MOOCs). These are free online college level courses available to students world-wide. As found in traditional classes, MOOCs are comprised of video recordings or podcasts of lectures and discussions by experts on various topics. Students can participate in live discussion boards and debates with fellow online classmates regarding their selected course. All of this may be accessed through any Internet-capable device, including smartphones and tablets.

The potential for MOOCs to extend higher education learning opportunities to massive audiences around the world is readily apparent. The *Wall Street Journal* reports that student participation rates are soaring at an amazing pace. "The largest provider, Coursera, has drawn five million, and nonprofit provider edX more than 1.3 million. And while the majority are still based in the U.S., their learners come from all over the globe: Among edX's students, 9% came from Africa and 12% from India." But, this means that thousands of students are taking the same course with the same instructor covering the exact same material. For some, this raises the question of sustainability of the traditional college model. Others, as noted in Lane and Kinser's article in *The Chronicle of Higher Education* are asking if we are embarking into the age of the "McDonaldization of Higher Education."

Since MOOCs generate no revenue, one quickly asks why schools are investing so heavily in the development of these courses. Some suggest it is to stay ahead of the technology curve. Faculty indicate that it is to supplement learning in traditional classes at the university, and to encourage participants to enroll in additional campus courses. Still others propose that the movement is in response to the fact that colleges and universities are facing tremendous pressures as families express valid concerns about the astronomical cost of a degree and the poor return on their investment. Schools experiencing enrollment loses are looking for ways to expand their base market and hope to reduce educational costs for students by developing online courses that are convenient, have an affordable fee, and offer college credit.

Many believe that America is on the cusp of a revolution in higher education based on this new technology. Although MOOCs have been around for a while, elite institutions such as Harvard, Princeton, Brown, Duke, Columbia, Sanford, University of Pennsylvania, University of Michigan, etc., are partnering with course development vendors at a breakneck speed. John Hennessey, President of Stanford, succinctly described the movement in an article by Ken Auletta in the *New Yorker*: "There's a tsunami coming." In a well-circulated article titled "The End of the University as We Know It," Nathan Harden sees the future in these terms:

> **In fifty years, if not much sooner, half of the roughly 4,500 colleges and universities now operating in the United States will have ceased to exist. The technology driving this change is already at work, and nothing can stop it. The future looks like this: Access to college-level education will be free for everyone; the residential college campus will become largely obsolete; tens of thousands of professors will lose their jobs; the bachelor's degree will become increasingly irrelevant; and ten years from now Harvard will enroll ten million students.**

Not everyone is on board that train. Although one could argue that the potential for MOOCs is impressive, some significant issues exist. In a *Wall Street Journal* article titled "An Early Report Card on Massive Open Online Courses," Geoffrey Fowler indicates that "often more than 90% of people who sign up for a MOOC don't finish, though many come to online learning with a different intent than would students at a traditional university." Research indicates that students need support and the personal touch in order to succeed in online courses. Although schools are using mentors and recorded audio comments to help students feel connected, "evidence is mounting that online learning doesn't work for all students. The Columbia study of Washington community college students found that all students performed less well in online courses than in face-to-face ones, but the gap was even wider among those with lower GPAs, men and African-Americans."

In her *New York Times* article, "The Year of the MOOC," Laura Pappano questions whether learning can be successfully ramped up on such a large scale. Grading is problematic in areas that involve writing and analysis, and cheating is rampant. "'We found groups of 20 people in a course submitting identical homework,' says David Patterson, professor at the University of California."

As time goes by, the overwhelming enthusiasm for the new technologies is becoming tempered, as exemplified by the insightful analysis of Janet Napolitano, President of the University of California:

> **I think there's a developing consensus that online learning is a tool for the tool box, where higher education is concerned; that it is not a silver bullet the way it was originally portrayed to be. It's a lot harder than it looks. And, by the way, if you do it right, it doesn't save all that much money, because you still have to have an opportunity for students to interact with either a teaching assistant or an assistant professor or professor at some level. And preparing the courses, if they're really going to be top-quality, is an investment as well.**

Add to this the fact that some professors are already objecting to technology teaching, feeling that true learning needs the interaction of classroom give-and-take between a student and a professor. In other words, how does one use the Socratic Method which sometimes uses an artificial adversarial technique to force the student to explain, or stretch learning and/or debating ability?

We must also remind ourselves that the wonderful technology of television was going to change education dramatically in the very early 1970s. It was called "The Sunrise Semester," and was claimed by many to revolutionize education. Then, as now, professors did not latch onto it en-mass for a number of reasons, one of them being self-preservation.

Higher Education's Dilemma

The high cost of college has prompted a variety of responses from our institutions, but so few of them are credible that it causes the public outcry to intensify rather than subside. The most pervasive response is, "Anecdotes! Please don't generalize based on examples." What is fascinating about this reaction is that the media uncovers a $600 toilet seat or a $400 hammer purchased by the Defense Department, and everyone, most especially our colleagues in higher education, believe the Defense Department is a sty full of waste. Yet mention an example of waste in higher education, and it becomes an anecdote, an exception to be dismissed. Bring up payments of over $300,000 for one speaker to visit the campus a few times, and it is an anecdote – not really indicative of the system. Mention a $50,000 soundproof chamber built for a professor who left the college before it was completed, and that's the price of quality.

If "anecdotes" does not suffice to defuse the concern, then "differences" might serve the purpose. Each college is different, so its pricing is different and its costs are different. What is ironic about this response is that some of us openly set the price in conformity with our little fleet and then pretend we are not shipmates. We compete for the same students, steal each other's renowned professors (sometimes by promising high salaries along with reduced teaching), offer the same programs, play on the same athletic field, vie for the same grants, obtain funds from the same foundations, yet pronounce our differences as the reason we are so expensive. Some years ago, as the heat was beginning to mount on colleges across the country, the National Institute of Independent Colleges and Universities put out its response to high cost in a document titled "The Truth About Costs in the Independent Sector of Higher Education."

Among its "truths" we find that "colleges that have endowments are using a large portion of the income from those endowments to support institutional aid programs and to keep tuition increases down." Yet increases the year the document was written were averaging two times the CPI. And the average amount of income used from endowment funds was less than the total income earned. Growing the endowment took precedent over reducing the tuition increase.

Another response is that "quality comes at a high price." Quality is and has long been the "in" word in higher education. Some institutions justify the ever-increasing high cost by the equipment they need – the computers, the technology, the library holdings, and a host of other academic-related items. The intent is to focus on high costs for expenses closely tied to the academic programs. Never is the exceptionally large administrative staff given as the reason, nor is the reduced teaching load announced in the president's letter informing the public about next year's tuition increases. What is absurd and ought to be understood by colleges' boards of trustees and by the legislatures and by the public is that all the reasons given under the guise of academic quality – library books, computers, increases in salary, lab equipment, technology, etc. – have been with us for decades, but only now do we haul them out and blame the high cost on them.

Is there a college in this country that, since its inception, did not have to wrestle with library holdings? Are salary increases a recent phenomenon? Lab equipment, especially in the '60s, was always a heavy budget item as we raced to the moon. And computers deserve a little respite as the current reason. We seem to forget that computers were sold under the false premise that costs would be reduced. It is worth repeating: Colleges always have been, and continue to be, labor-intensive institutions. If we add nonteaching staff and if we reduce teaching loads for our faculty, the tuition will always go up at unusually high rates. If economists can agree on anything, it is that reduced productivity will drive up costs. All the costs of providing a quality education have always been with us. They have become unreasonable during the last four decades. No one would dispute that Harvard University is an institution that personifies quality; more than this, among American institutions, it always has been top-of-the-line. The same is true with Stanford; it is a university that also is classified as a place of quality and has long enjoyed that reputation. Both have been pacesetters for many of the rest to follow. In 1970–71, when both of these institutions were considered among the very best, when both were models of quality, Harvard had a tuition of $2,600, while Stanford charged $2,400. These rates were comparable to those of many private colleges throughout the country and, when measured against average family income, were less than one-third. For the year 1987–88, Harvard went up to $11,390, and Stanford was at $11,208 in tuition alone. At present they both exceed the $60,000-a-year range for room, board, and tuition (as are so many other private colleges), and this is more than the average family income.

The increases remain larger than twice the CPI, yet the blame cannot be laid at the feet of the goddess called "Quality." They were top-drawer then; they are top-drawer now. The unusually large increases at these two schools, and countless others, are not due to all the things we in colleges have had to face for years – from high heating and cooling costs (which was the reason given for large increases during the oil embargo, when oil ran high, but was forgotten when oil prices dropped to one-half of what they had been) to new equipment to salary increases to new fringe benefits to more books for our library, many of which, like computers and eBooks, have actually lowered in price. No, the reasons for high costs have more to do with Drucker's observation, which bears repeating: "Unless challenged, every organization tends to become slack, easy going, diffuse."

Connecticut College, under the theme of quality, gave as its defense a very low student/faculty ratio accompanied by a paid sabbatical every four years. It pointed out that most colleges give paid sabbaticals every seven years, but their notion of quality was to allow the professors paid leave after every fourth year. The more one analyzes this college's definition of quality, the closer one gets to the ironic conclusion that keeping the professors away from students is a very active and worthwhile goal. And judging from the tuition, they are succeeding.

Only in academia do we define quality in terms of fewer hours available to do what we are paid to do.

> **Evidently, we think of ourselves as rare pieces of art: The less available we are, the more valuable we become.**

Indeed, one of the conclusions arrived at from a high powered Council for Advancement and Support of Education (CASE) Senior Seminar was, "To publicize freezing or trimming of departmental budgets, for example, can prove hazardous because of faculty sensitivities and also because the public may perceive such cuts as a reduction in quality or scope of academic programs." Clearly we often are driven more by marketing considerations than by substantive ones.

Some time ago, the Association of Governing Boards of Universities and Colleges (AGB) had invested a lot of money and time producing a booklet called "9 Myths and Truth About Tuitions," a piece designed to "help" us show the public why the costs of higher education continue to escalate at rates that far exceed the inflationary trends. The piece made mention of the high cost of heat some 10 years after the last oil embargo. A fascinating document sent to all members of the National Association of Independent Colleges and Universities (NAICU) outlined six suggestions on how to reply to the expected media blast that would result from the latest large tuition hike. It cited the expected reasons, such as salary increases, aid to students, equipment purchases, and building maintenance, all of which have been part and parcel of financial budgeting since our first college started on American soil in 1636. Only one reason cited has the ring of truth: increased student services such as security and career planning. Overall, they represent a small portion of the increase, but they do give us an excuse that we disproportionately exaggerate.

Virtually all college presidents and higher-education organizations that are defensive about high tuition increases lament the connection made between the Consumer Price Index and running a college. Their reports and letters emphatically deny any connection citing as proof that we are labor-intensive—which we are. Then they go on to blame salary increases, equipment, maintenance, and other aspects of college life, not realizing the inherent contradiction they create for themselves. First of all, colleges have always been labor-intensive, and salaries and increases have always been of major concern. Why have they become the problem, unless, of course, we have added far more people than needed? The same can be said of equipment and building maintenance, both of which have always been a major concern.

Finally, if running a college and the CPI have no relationship, then how about comparing the increased cost of college with the growth in family income. Should not a labor-intensive education "business" approximately reflect the average growth of real income for society as a whole? Unfortunately, college costs have outpaced real income, making even that comparison a disaster. The real problem for colleges is that the cost of not one business, service, enterprise, agency, or medical plan has risen as fast and for such an extended period as has higher education—both private and public.

Solutions

We have allowed the waste and nonfeasance to accumulate over a long period of time—almost four decades—and getting our financial house in order will not be done overnight, nor will it be done without a strong determination to do so. Playing at it won't work, and there will be resistance. You can be the judge of whether or not many of our colleges are on the level, or whether they play games as it suits their purposes. Suppose you read the headlines: "Colleges Seek to Raise Record Sums of Money to Battle Inflation, Hold Students, and Survive." The story unfolds:

> **Alumni, beware. Chances are your college will soon starting hitting you for more money than ever. But parents of collegians, take heart: many colleges plan to use part of the money to curb tuition increases. Institutions across the country are planning, or have begun, fundraising drives on an unprecedented scale.**

The article goes on to name one university after another that will be seeking huge endowments to offset much-needed tuition increases, including a little 850-student college that is hoping to raise $23 million. "In addition, state and local institutions are seeking private money more avidly than in the past," says one university president. "The way inflation looks, we simply won't be able to go to families and ask for that much more tuition. Expenses have increased 9 percent a year, but the university could not, in good judgment, raise tuition more than 6 percent a year," he says with the sincerity of an 8-year-old just before Christmas. "Fortunately, we already have all the buildings we need."

In chimes the head of the Association of American Colleges. "Every college is terribly concerned. The competition is going to become keener and keener ... and the matter of cost will become more important. Colleges see endowments as a means to hold down costs to students."

Other college presidents join the choir claiming that the new endowment goals are for people and programs; the physical plant is up to snuff, they say, no new buildings are needed. And finally, as the curtain closes and the music fades, we hear the final refrain: "Federal cutbacks are a part of the problem, so we must raise endowment to keep tuition below the rate of inflation."

What is fascinating, frustrating, and deeply deceptive, is that the story is from a national news piece and is dated *December 29, 1975*. Not 1989 or 2013, but 1975. Deceptive, because this happens to be the period in which tuition increases started their unrelenting charge to the top. Fascinating, because the first university president quoted is the same one whose university, as mentioned earlier, had raised its tuition unconscionably in order to attract a better cut of student. Frustrating, because it shows how self-serving so many of our colleges have become, and how marketing has a tight grip on them. Our goal was not to hold tuition down, as we promised our benefactors, but to build our endowment.

In the fall of 1988, one of our public universities, sensing that it was not in the top 20 of its desired peer group, gathered all its resources for a $200 million campaign so it could be "ranked." Most of the money went to people, which is not bad, until we read that the "people" are a few professors selected for multimillion-dollar endowed chairs, which means limited teaching, if any at all. It is referred to as "hiring a star." Of course, part of the negotiations consists of reducing the teaching – sometimes none – for the "star." The irony continues year after year; the colleges most successful at raising money have increased their cost and their tuition the most.

Or consider the public report of a professor who had an insider's view of what his ivy covered college did in response to their vaunted business school being dropped from the top tier, as ranked by some journal. For about a year the college lamented, worried, debated, and decided to spend a large amount of money in a marketing appeal. No changes were made in the program; only more marketing took place. Lo and behold, they did the right thing. The very next year they were inserted in the top tier. Who says colleges are not businesses?

***

The first step in addressing the deep-rooted problem of college costs is to reformulate the governing boards of both private and public colleges and universities. Presidents serve, on average, about seven years at any one institution. This means there is ample turnover in our more than 3,600 colleges in any one year. The governing board must tell all applicants that one of their primary roles is to hold down costs, and be emphatic about it. Simply put, the new president and the board have to be on the same page.

They must have a similar view on financial matters, broadly defined. This is an area where board members, many chosen because of their extensive financial backgrounds, can lend strong expertise to the institution. If the board and president are not committed to the effort, then we can expect more business as usual, and the continued financial excess accompanied by its high cost will remain with us.

Conventional wisdom says board members should remain no longer than a term or two, about three to six years, and then new blood is needed. This method, practiced by most colleges, is wrong. A board meets very infrequently, about four to six times a year, and while most members will tell you the real work goes on in committees or that the board meetings are long, two-day affairs, what they don't say, or don't know, is that a lot of "show and tell" is going on. Some matters are pretty well-baked before they even see them. Presidents aren't fools; if they want to impress the board, they wheel out a professor or two who has done outstanding research, leaving the board with the impression that all the professors are similarly engaged. Then they report that teaching loads must go down and tuition go up because that's the price of quality. They hasten to add that some of the colleges in their little "cohort" are already at nine credits per semester, or six, and to remain competitive they also should reduce the teaching load. They never call it less teaching per se; they use the subterfuge of more research.

Boards generally have to depend on their president, and in so doing, pay attention to what the president brings to the board. It would be far better if board members had longer terms on the board so that they could see the same prof doing the same research wheeled out five years later. They would then be in a better position to ask more penetrating questions about the rest of the faculty; they would have a longer perspective of continuing events at the college. If board members had more longevity, they could remind the president that tuition increases have been extraordinarily large year after year, always explained by "that's the price of quality, and we must stay in line with our peer group, but next year we should achieve our goal, and reasonable increases will be restored." Long-term board members remember past events and promises. Outsiders cannot appreciate the fact that a board member does not become conversant and knowledgeable about the sometimes byzantine ways of a college for a number of years. And just about then it's time for new blood!

To steer a steady course toward responsible financial behavior, our governing boards, which bear the ultimate responsibility and authority, whether private or public, should allow their membership the time needed to learn about the college and to understand its president's recommendations with a longer sense of history. The board need not involve itself in day-to-day affairs, nor should it interfere with the real leadership expected from the president. But neither should its members be rotated out just when understanding and some real input, based on longer experience, begin. With a board whose membership is constantly changing, one can begin to understand why it is easier to give in to the countless requests for everything under the sun rather than ask the probing and experienced questions. Longevity of greater than six or seven years is needed by both board members and presidents. Colleges are not like military bases, where a manual for just about everything is available so that a three year tour of duty at one is pretty much the same as at another. College accountability occurs over a longer period of time because implementation of ideas and changes are much slower.

Boards of trustees are the place where just about all recommendations are decided. And while it is natural for boards of public as well as private institutions, to want to support their president, they must ask the difficult questions and make the difficult decisions. They have not done so with reductions of faculty teaching; they have not done so with large increases in the nonteaching staff; and they have not done so as far as tuition is concerned. They have not forcefully made a connection between the increased cost and teaching reductions and increased administration. They have allowed the president to offer excuse after excuse as to why they must increase costs at twice the rate of inflation ... year after year after year.

The president of the institution is the person most responsible for the budgetary woes we have. No governing board ever forced a president to waste money, to lower productivity, to add layers of bureaucracy. Given the financially conservative nature of most board members, it's a tribute to the president's persuasive powers that many colleges have become fat around the middle. The burden of keeping the budget in line falls most heavily on the president, hopefully with a strong and experienced board in the background.

***

Why are administrations so large? Quite simply because it is the administration that makes the decision on how large it should be. If they have decided to be oversized, as so many have, only the president is to blame. The president's powers are not absolute – far from it – but the president does have a strong arm when it comes to the size of the college's administration. We've all seen large administrations that were geared up to make the system work better, to serve the student better, but because of their size, they sometimes become an obstacle and a hindrance to satisfaction. A large administration becomes imbued and entranced with rules, regulations, policies, and the omnipresent manual, each of which inevitably gains a life of its own and weighs us down with a system of processes and appeals that better serve the bureaucracy than the individual.

One of the benefits of a lean administration is that it allows each administrator the leeway to make decisions and to be responsible for them. Accountability is much easier and much more desired by administrators who want to develop a solution or help solve someone's problem. With a lean administration, response time is improved because the standard excuse of "so and so was handling that" is eliminated. There is no one else to shuck the work or decision onto. Granted, sometimes the daily work schedule gets heavy, but the changing seasons of campus life – breaks and summer – allow for planning, catch-up, and a slower pace when it is needed. A lean administration allows people to get to know students and faculty on a face-to-face basis.

It is a fact, though not often acknowledged publicly, that faculty and upper administration are often at odds with one another. Faculty governance and administration often collide. Too much time is spent doing battle over inconsequential items that soon grow out of importance and end up wasting time and energy that could be spent on more beneficial educational affairs.

The president's job is essential, and often determines the direction the college takes. The faculty are the academic officers of the institution and should be involved deeply in just about all education matters, including research. In what sounds like a paradoxical statement, presidents of every college, large or small, should teach a course in their specialty. While it takes some time away from other efforts, it ends up saving time by eliminating misunderstandings that result from the perception that faculty teach and everyone else administers. As the kids say, many good vibes will accompany this action, along with the message that classroom teaching is important, even at so-called research institutions.

The students were on the march, a protest was in order. However, the leaders of the protest were students that I taught the year before. Pleasant conversations replaced the protest. Fair resolution replaced a nasty conflict whereby the students might be dealing with an unknown face. Whether dean, vice president, or president, the students and especially the faculty should know and see you!

The final, and by far the most crucial reason why a lean administration is so important on a college campus is because it is the only way to improve on faculty productivity. We cannot expect faculty to entertain the notion of restoring a more respectable teaching load if the clear perception is that the administration is bloated. Too many faculty think the administrative salaries are too high, which, generally speaking, is not true, but it is accurate that there are too many administrative positions at all levels on the typical college campus.

The high cost of college is neither simple nor can it be explained in a sentence. Nevertheless, we are often asked what is the one thing colleges can do to cut costs, or at least bring the tuition increases into the real world? The answer is direct. Reduce the size of the administration. Only when the administration is downsized can we then address the classroom productivity of faculty. With a lean administration, we can then begin to address the terribly difficult situation of low productivity on the part of faculty members. Without a lean administration, the job is impossible. It cannot be overstated: faculty are one of the most important engines, if not the most important engine that drives the college. Of course, good, strong leadership within the administration is a necessity, but the impact of administration on all aspects of faculty involvement is weakened when it grows itself into a bureaucracy. The vitality and cooperation of the faculty are always enhanced if they have confidence in their leadership, rather than distrust, distance, and speculative notions of what is going on behind closed and crowded doors.

***

Reductions in normal teaching load need to be examined. Originally they occurred because a handful of faculty members really needed a reduction for substantial research. Others coattailed their reduction until everyone had it and it became the sine qua non of the institution. Other institutions saw what their supposed peers were doing and, under the guise of "quality," jumped aboard. Listen to the new president of a California university outline his plan to make his institution the pre-eminent public urban place of learning: "Both to ensure our ability to hire new faculty into this university and to enable continuing faculty to meet our expanding mandate, we must do something about workload. A 12-credit teaching load limits the time our faculty can spend advising students, working in the community, and enriching their own knowledge and that of their students through research, scholarly activities, and creative expression. It also makes our institution less competitive with institutions of comparable quality and mission."

His comments are probably sincere and may curry favor with the faculty, but it is certain they will cost everyone more than necessary, from taxpayer to student. And it reduces the work of faculty without any decrease in compensation. We must all be careful in assuming that faculty are created equal; that all are capable of doing seminal research; and that great benefits will only accrue to student and society if all faculty do less teaching. It is undeniable, however, that there are great researchers at some of our campuses, and reduced teaching is imperative for them.

There is a system that eliminates the "one size fits all" mentality, and it is quite simple. Allow each department a number of "reduction from teaching" credits. Let the department, through its chair, decide who gets the reduction and for how long. Someone finishing a book or project may get some reduction for a period, and then the reduction is passed along to a different person who is in need of more time for research. Only the most meaningful scholarly work, as determined by the department, would deserve the reduction. With a fixed number of "reduction credits," the department is forced to determine whose research is most urgent and most important.

Let's remember, higher education, for at least the last century, was designed to leave faculty with free time for advising students, delving into scholarship and new learning, and research. It has been roughly the last four decades that have seen us reduce teaching time for faculty with a competitive vengeance. And costs have risen accordingly. It cannot be overstated: college faculty are not overpaid; they are underworked. The elusive silver bullet to solve the cost problem does exist – indeed, two of them: reduce all nonteaching staff, and restore a normal teaching load for faculty. And when the reduction for heavy duty research is allocated to another professor, the full teaching load returns to the initial professor.

Additional Solutions

There are additional cost saving devices, but none measures up to the above two. One would be to schedule classes in a tighter array, more to satisfy the student rather than the professor. For example, if 25 sections of an introductory English class are scheduled, each to hold no more than 20 students, than the total capacity would be 500 students. But if only 400 students were available, we could make do with five fewer sections. It's a cost-income system that has been used at a few colleges and allows for tighter scheduling without increasing the size of the class. One of the great benefits is that it allows the department to decide if and when to run lightly enrolled higher-level classes.

In clearer words, if departments know there will be a few under-enrolled courses (e.g., courses within a major that a handful of students need to take in order to graduate), the chairs have it within their power to schedule them simply because the total number of multiple classes has been expeditiously predetermined. No need to wrestle with the dean over cutting under-enrolled classes; if the department has been diligent with its total number of classes, there is leeway for a small number of under-enrolled sections. This is a "cost/income system" developed for a very few colleges, and further refined to include administrative units within the college. Indeed, a very deliberate cost/income system can be designed to control administrative bloat, with the extremely important side effect of showing the faculty that controlling costs is a full-team effort. Once operational and its advantages are understood by all, it can be used with great success.

For relatively easy to follow details of a successful (controlling costs and increasing department control of its program) cost/income system, go to Postscript 2.

***

Another cost-saving step would be for the NCAA (National Collegiate Athletic Association) and colleges to eliminate Division II. As mentioned, there are currently three divisions. The top one is already split into a large Division I and a small Division 1-AA, and they both allow many athletic scholarships (the Ivies excepted). In a sense, they are the farm team for the pros in some sports. The middle conference, Division II is in never-never land – too weak to make money, not strong enough to gain exposure, too costly to be of much benefit. A few of these schools could go up to Division 1, and the majority should go down to Division III.

***

Groups that can influence and help bring down college costs are state and federal legislators, foundations, and citizen contributors which would include all alumni. Legislators must ask the tough questions before allocating large amounts of money to public institutions that do not practice effective cost containment. Sample surveys should be conducted to determine whether or not there has been an extraordinary increase in nonteaching staff. Also, there should be an audit of the true teaching load – as opposed to the stated official version. Why has the semester been shortened from the traditional 17 weeks to 14 weeks (including exam week) at many schools? Our government, both at the state and federal levels, must extend to higher education a greater degree of financial benign neglect. They must stop thinking that we in higher education are in dire financial straits – quite the opposite. Our coffers are, for the most part, full or amply supplied, and our endowments are growing and always in search of more. Foundations, before awarding large grants for specific projects, should question the ever-rising tuition rates of the college. Just mentioning an interest in burgeoning tuition will get beneficial results, and many colleges must be made aware that derelict costing strategies have consequences.

***

Alumni and other contributors should let the colleges know that their hard-earned contributions should help drive down costs, not increase them. Contributors can and should speak with a louder and more directed voice. When they are asked to contribute toward a new building on campus, they should question whether or not tuition will be lower because no tuition will be used to build the new building. Contributors can be a powerful force in holding down tuition increases. Their influence is essential. Naming buildings after them is fine, as is 'named' scholarship funds. Virtually any help they give their alma mater is most welcome. But they have to express their view on the continued high costs of attending. Better yet, they have to challenge the president on his or her reasons, many of which are fictitious.

***

Everyone knows that the federal government provides a tremendous amount of money to just about all of our colleges and universities. The federal government should provide disincentives for all colleges that provide government-backed loans, yet continue to increase costs beyond the public's cost of living. We also know that our public elementary and secondary education system within virtually every city limit, from pre-kindergarten on up, is in dire straits. Yet we continue excessively funding all colleges, many of which have enormous or very large endowments, super high tuition and fees, and showcase campuses. Our priorities are confusing.

> **We pay too little attention to the cracks in the foundation of our education system and too much financial attention polishing the dome of our rich and solidly-footed campus steeples.**

How to Find Schools that Offer the Biggest Bang for the Buck

The case has been made that far too many colleges and universities burn through mounds of cash with little to show for it, while some others use their resources effectively to educate students at a relatively low cost and still provide a first-class education. If you're in the market for a college education, how do you identify those schools that operate most efficiently? Finding those institutions with the lowest sticker prices is relatively easy. However, finding the college that provides the best value specifically for you is another matter altogether.

> **Using the car analogy, is a Ferrari a cost-effective purchase? Well, if you're going to use it to commute to work or go grocery shopping, maybe not so much – a Chevy Cruze may be a better choice. If you're a sports car enthusiast with lots of extra cash and a lust for horsepower, maybe the Ferrari is a great buy. It's a very personal decision. That's why college rankings, for the most part, are irrelevant.**

Beyond any doubt, all college ranking lists are very subjective. The rankings are based on values that may apply to a certain group of individuals, but not to others. Even changing the arbitrary weights assigned to the various values will drastically alter the results. Just as people have different ideas about their favorite actors and songs, it is important that a list of colleges reflects your choices and priorities. This exercise allows the reader to arrange the easily accessible data in ways that will match your own personal interests, values and concerns.

There is an incredible amount of information available about postsecondary institutions in the United States. However, we must again emphasize that all rankings, lists, survey data and guidebooks have serious weakness and should be cautiously used only to whittle down the amazing number of choices to a manageable short list of schools that can then be looked at more closely.

As mentioned earlier in the book, much of the information used in college rankings is provided by schools themselves. This often results in the expected tendency for colleges and universities to favor their own institution with the rankings. Data can be manipulated or arranged in ways that serve their own interests, known as "gaming the system." For example, a college may aggressively solicit applications from students who do not meet admission standards and subsequently are not accepted into the institution. This results in a lot more applications, accompanied with a larger number of student rejections, thereby giving the college a higher ranking. In some cases it might move the college from a 'selective' rank to a 'very selective' rank. Some institutions include incomplete applications in their data reports, which also serve to lower the acceptance rate. *The Chronicle of Higher Education* reports another recent dilemma:

> **Over the last decade, the proliferation of no-fee "fast track" applications has made counting an even iffier exercise. If a student sends back an application pre-populated with data, should a college count that application? Heck yeah, some deans have told me in response to such questions. No way, others have said. Who's right?**

Lavish spending, even if it is misguided, can raise a college's standing. Bob Morse of *U.S. News & World Report*'s Best Colleges indicates that "the average spending per student on instruction, student services, academic support, research, and related educational expenditures... has a weight of 10 percent in the overall rankings." Yet, years of experience shows that not all of the money spent is for the benefit of the students.

Some factors typically used in many college rankings have no evidence to support that there is any measureable impact on student academic outcomes. For example, a higher ratio of full-time faculty usually means a better ranking for the college. However, The Delta Cost Project found that there is no consistent research to support the notion that access to full-time faculty enhances student learning or degree attainment. In fact, a report released in September, 2013 by the National Bureau of Economic Research concluded that part-time faculty are actually better teachers than tenured professors in introductory courses at Northwestern University.

Guidebooks often use peer assessment to determine program quality. *U.S. News & World Report* evaluates "Best Undergraduate Teaching" institutions based on the results of a peer assessment survey in which college presidents, provosts and admissions deans were asked to nominate colleges "that are committed to undergraduate teaching." Those schools receiving the highest number of nominations made the "Best" list. In other words, the quality of teaching at a particular school was determined by asking administrators at other institutions how effective the teaching is at other than their school. Would you assess the quality of automotive repair service at a particular repair shop by surveying managers and sales persons at other competing repair shops?

Teacher-faculty ratios can also be misleading. Many high ranking colleges and universities have low student/faculty ratios. However, they are often schools where high research and publication expectations are placed on the faculty. Thus, the professors there tend to teach fewer courses compared to those at schools where research is less prevalent and effective teaching is prized.

Then too, we have the issue of average salaries after graduation. Some rankings publish an annual ROI (return on investment) rate by calculating 30-year earnings divided by total costs of college. Let's take a closer look at that by comparing a graduate of California Institute of Technology (Caltech), which is ranked near the top of the Forbes "Colleges with the Best Return on Investment" list, and one from Mount Vernon Nazarene University, which falls closer to the bottom. The ROI figure does not take into account the talents, academic skills, and intellect of the student attending Caltech vs. enrollees at a lower-ranked school. Is it possible there could be a significant difference in the aptitude, academic proficiency, and employment network connections of students attending these very different institutions? Also, some of the salary averages are based on an extremely small sample of graduates, raising serious validity concerns.

Freshmen-to-sophomore retention rates, the percentage of students who return after their freshmen year, are frequently used as a key measurement in the college ranking process. The schools with high grading standards may be penalized by not inflating the scores of poorly performing students. Institutions that traditionally admit marginal students also suffer in the rankings since they tend to experience a greater number of dropouts compared to colleges with more restrictive admission policies. This holds true even if the less selective schools are highly successful at nurturing better performers than would normally be expected from the populations they serve. In other words, does giving marginal students a chance to prove themselves hurt the very school that tries to help?

Similarly, four-year graduation rates are commonly used in ranking criteria, and on the surface it seems like a reasonable consideration. But, one must question if highly rated institutions are simply benefitting from the result of the "elite in, elite out" syndrome, perhaps more than their commitments to advising and preparing potential graduates.

The list goes on and on, but let's just say that the college ranking data is questionable. Like making sausage, the final product may be appealing, but viewing the process can be unappetizing. Regardless, college rankings and search programs may serve a very useful purpose. They provide detailed data in one convenient location and, although data collection methodology can be criticized, efforts are made to ensure that statistics are reported consistently. Without these data-gathering organizations, figures generated by individual institutions would be questionable and an unfathomable bag of numbers.

Rankings can suggest topics that need to be researched in greater detail and can generate helpful ideas that may not have been previously considered by the student or parents. They can help you focus in on your abilities, talents, and priorities to generate a list of colleges that will meet your specific requirements. Good cost-effective schools that were not on the radar screen may appear as viable options. Furthermore, your eyes may be opened with enlightening information about those places you already had in mind. Finally, college rankings can sometimes positively influence institutions to improve mission-critical weaknesses identified through the process. Yes, it's an imperfect system, but a fine place to start a college search.

The good news is that there are many lists of "affordable" colleges and universities. Some of the more well-known ones are U.S. News & World Report's *Ultimate College Guide*, *The College Board handbook* and *The Best Colleges by the Princeton Review*, which can be purchased at the local bookstore. They may provide some assistance. Some of them identify the top 10, 25, or 100 low-cost institutions. That's all well and good if you're looking for colleges across the nation that may include institutions in New Mexico, Massachusetts, South Dakota and Hawaii. Others narrow down the geographic range by region or categories of institutional type.

Practically speaking, most college-bound students can't consider all of the institutions spread throughout the United States or even within a widespread region. They are restricted by a whole lot of variables such as cost, geographic range, choice of major, graduation rates, internship opportunities, etc., and need to make comparisons of schools within a specific set of guidelines. Still, for those who want to begin narrowing down their choices by costs, there are plenty of resources that can help.

Step 1 – Use free online college search engines

Rather than spent the time and money to buy magazines or guidebooks, students and parents can obtain all the background information they need to make an informed choice through a myriad number of free online search engines. Again, keep in mind that these sites have strengths and pitfalls and should be viewed with a dose of skepticism. Below, listed in alphabetical order, are some of the most common online resources. The specific web addresses are available in the corresponding chapter references section at the end of the book. If you're uncertain about where to start, three widely-used general search engines are the *National Center for Education Statistics College Navigator, The College Board Big Future* and *College Confidential*.

> *AffordableCollegesOnline*
> *CNN Money How Much Will that College Really Cost*
> *CNN Money's Colleges with the Highest-Paid Grads*
> *The Chronicle of Higher Education College Completion*
> *College Board Big Future College Search*
> *CollegeCalc College Price Rankings*
> *College Confidential College Search*
> *CollegeData College Match*
> *CollegeXpress*
> *College InSight*

College Prowler
CollegeStats.org
eduLaunchpad.com How to Search Colleges
FastWeb College Search
Kiplinger Best Values in Public Colleges
NerdScholar
PayScale College Education ROI Rankings
Peterson's College Search
SuperMatch College Search
U.S. Department of Education College Affordability and Transparency Center
U.S. Department of Education College Navigator
U.S. Department of Education College Scorecard
U.S. Department of Education IPEDS Data Center
U.S. News & World Report's Best Value Schools
Washington Monthly College Guide
What Will They Learn?

Sticker Price – Tuition and Fees

If you want to begin your search by identifying the lowest priced institutions, *FastWeb* can provide quick access to a hierarchical listing of schools by sticker costs, in your area (click on the "colleges" tab, then select "college search"). You can search within a specified radius of your zip code up to 500 miles, or by state.

Another comprehensive listing of postsecondary schools by tuition and fee cost alone is available on the Web-based *U.S. Department of Education College Affordability and Transparency Center*. It identifies the lowest and highest tuition rates by various institutional categories within the United States. At the bottom of the home page is a link that allows the reader to download the data file of all institutions used to generate the listings. After clicking on that link, a spreadsheet appears. Clicking on the "tuition" tab at the bottom of the page brings up a list of over 4,200 postsecondary schools that can be sorted by public or private, lowest to highest 2013-14 tuition and fee charges, or alphabetically, by name or state.

College Board Big Future College Search can also provide a listing of schools in the United States by in-state tuition and fees that may be sorted by region or state. This site identifies the following four-year colleges with the lowest and highest 2013 in-state tuition and required fee rates in the nation:

Four-Year Colleges with the Lowest In-State Tuition and Required Fee Rates

1. Oglala Lakota College, Kyle, SD, Tuition/fees: $2,900
2. Holy Trinity Orthodox Seminary, Jordanville, NY, Tuition/fees: $3,000
3. Institute of American Indian Arts, Santa Fe, NM, Tuition/fees: $3,600
4. South Georgia State College, Douglas, GA, Tuition/fees: $3,626
5. Sinte Gleska University, Mission, SD, Tuition/fees: $3,800
6. Global University, Springfield, MO, Tuition/fees: $3,870
7. Dalton State College, Dalton, GA, Tuition/fees: $3,910
8. Middle Georgia State College, Macon, GA, Tuition/fees: $3,910
9. New Mexico Highlands University, Las Vegas, NM, Tuition/fees: $4,000
10. World College, Virginia Beach, VA, Tuition/fees: $4,150

Four-Year Colleges with the Highest In-State Tuition and Required Fee Rates

1. Columbia University, New York, NY ($49,138)
2. Sarah Lawrence College, Bronxville, NY ($48,696)
3. Vassar College, Poughkeepsie, NY ($47,890)
4. Carnegie Mellon University, Pittsburgh, PA ($47,642)
5. Trinity College, Hartford, CT ($47,560)
6. Columbia University: School of General Studies, New York, NY ($47,511)
7. George Washington University, Washington, DC ($47,343)

8. Wesleyan University, Middletown, CT ($47,244)
9. Tulane University, New Orleans, LA ($46,930)
10. Bucknell University, Lewisburg, PA ($46,902)

Average Net Price

Another way of evaluating costs is by subtracting the average amount of institutional and government grants and scholarships students receive, from the cost of attendance. The result is the average net cost. The trick here is that this is an "average" figure. As discussed in the Chapter 6 regarding tuition discounting, schools with an average freshmen discount rate of 50% may have some students enjoying a 90% reduction while less qualified students are receiving a 10% discount – or perhaps none at all. They pay the full listed amount. The net price you pay is very specific to your circumstances and the college's aid policies. This will be discussed in greater detail in the following chapter. The *U.S. Department of Education College Affordability and Transparency Center* identifies the following four-year schools with the lowest and highest 2010-11 academic year net costs:

<u>Four-Year Colleges with the Lowest Average Net Costs</u>

1. Berea College, Berea, KY (-$20,746)
2. Family of Faith College, Shawnee , OK (-$5,585)
3. The University of Texas-Pan American, Edinburg, TX ($-95)
4. South Texas College, McAllen, TX (-$85)
5. Elizabeth City State University, Elizabeth City, NC ($909)
6. Indian River State College, Fort Pierce, FL ($1,440)
7. Sitting Bull College, Fort Yates, ND ($1,694)
8. Texas A&M University-Texarkana, Texarkana, TX ($1,923)
9. Bais Medrash Elyon, Monsey, New York ($2,205)
10. Hobe Sound Bible College, Hobe Sound, FL ($2,250)

<u>Four-Year Colleges with the Highest Average Net Costs</u>

1. American University of Health Sciences, Signal Hill, CA ($64,465)
2. Pacific College of Oriental Medicine, New York, NY ($49,670)
3. School of the Art Institute of Chicago, Chicago, IL ($42,882)
4. Southwest University of Visual Arts, Albuquerque, NM ($40,904)
5. Southwest University of Visual Arts, Tucson, AZ ($40,332)
6. Ringling College of Art and Design, Sarasota, FL ($40,222)
7. The Boston Conservatory, Boston, MA ($39,602)
8. Berklee College of Music, Boston, MA ($38,814)
9. California Institute of the Arts, Valencia, CA ($38,802)
10. School of Visual Arts, New York, NY ($37,884)

Historical Tuition Rate Increases

Another cost factor to consider is the percentage of tuition and fee increases over several years. These figures are available for individual schools at *CollegeCalc* and *The U.S. Department of Education College Affordability and Transparency Center*. Comparative average figures are presented to help provide an indication of expected charges in the future. *The U.S. Department of Education College Affordability and Transparency Center* identifies the following four-year schools with the lowest and highest tuition and fees changes between 2009 and 2011:

<u>Four-Year Colleges with the Lowest Rate of Tuition Increases</u>

1. Horizon College San Diego, San Diego, CA (-62.8%)
2. Colorado Heights University, Denver, CO (-61.4%)
3. Columbia College, Columbia, MO (-58.6%)
4. Baptist Bible College and Graduate School, Springfield, MO (-49.5%)
5. Daniel Webster College, Nashua, NH (-47.5%)

6. Stevens-Henager College-Ogden, Ogden, UT (-46.9%)
7. Herzing University-Toledo, Toledo, OH (-32.4%)
8. University of Northwestern Ohio, Lima, OH (-31.8%)
9. Herzing University-Madison, Madison, WI (-27.6%)
10. Potomac College-Herndon, Herndon, VA (-27.1%)

Four-Year Colleges with the Highest Rate of Tuition Increases

1. Moody Bible Institute, Chicago, IL (458.4%)
2. South Texas College, McAllen, TX (140.2%)
3. American Baptist College, Nashville, TN (79.0%)
4. Boston Baptist College, Boston, MA (67.9%)
5. Bethel College, Hampton, VA (60.9%)
6. Augusta State University, Augusta, GA (53.9%)
7. College of Coastal Georgia, Brunswick, GA (51.9%)
8. Tri-State Bible College, South Point, OH (51.2%)
9. Texas A&M University-Texarkana, Texarkana, TX (47.3%)
10. Boston Architectural College, Boston, MA (46.7%)

Step 2 – Narrow the field to ten or so colleges by identifying other essential factors

In nearly all cases, it makes the most sense to narrow down college choices on a variety of criteria in addition to financial considerations. Five of the more essential criteria include:

Geographic Location

You may find a wonderful, cost-effective college four states away, but the inconvenience and additional travelling expenses may not be worth it. What does the surrounding area have to offer? Is it important to be close to home? How close? *College Confidential College Search* provides an option for identifying schools located in great college towns.

Size

Colleges range in size from under 100 students to over 60,000. They each present academic and social benefits and disadvantages. Smaller schools may offer more personal attention, less bureaucracy and more opportunities to collaborate with professors. Larger institutions tend to offer a wider range of academic choices and student activities, state-of-the-art research facilities, famous faculty, and well-funded sports programs. Students need to focus on what feels right for them as individuals.

Admissions Selectivity

Harvard may be an appealing choice, but if you're heaps away from meeting the academic entrance requirements, it's a moot point. *The College Board Big Future* site identifies the following five admission range options:

> Open admission (all or most admitted)
> Less selective (75% or more admitted)
> Somewhat selective (50-75% admitted)
> Very selective (25-50% admitted)
> Most selective (less than 25% admitted

It may be worth mentioning that a study of law school grads found "the salary boost for achieving high grades more than makes up for the salary depreciation associated with attending a lower-ranked school." In other words, it may be worth identifying colleges where the student has a better chance of performing well, as opposed to overreaching to a higher profile institution where competition among students is stiff and good grades harder to come by. Mr. Carey, director of the New America Foundation's Education Policy Program, presents this perspective:

> **Everyone knows that's a good school because smart people go there, and smart people go there because it's a good school – and also irrelevant to the bulk of students, who aren't going to an elite institution**

Major

There is usually no urgency for most students to decide upon a major at this early stage. Besides, most college students change their major after discovering courses they find to be appealing and motivating. A typical example is Taylor, a good student, but she was not fond of her history professor. For sure, she was not going into history. As the semester progressed, she began to like history, and said what any professor likes to hear, "He's the best!" She changed her major to history, and upon graduation will make one great history teacher.

However, learning about majors now can help you make good decisions later. You want to be sure that a college is likely to offer the general fields of study that may be of interest. Some majors, like nursing and engineering, may require an early commitment because of the high demand and advance time needed to enroll in all of the required courses.

Personal Fit

An important step in finding the right college for you is to look carefully at yourself. Parents and friends can help you. Ask yourself, "Am I a big city person or do I really like the small town?" If you like the hustle and bustle of the city, along with the type student it attracts (remember, your roommate may be a fast mover), then, by all means put New York University or Temple University, or any one of many city-located schools on your list. If you like the quiet setting of a small college, then Gettysburg College, Lycoming, or Amherst, or any of literally hundreds of choices should go on your list. If you want a location near the big city, but not in it, there are hundreds, such as York College or Willamette, from which to choose.

If you are half decent in sports, not great but good, and want to continue playing, then look for a Division III school, perhaps a Division II, but don't expect Ohio State to be too welcoming. Spend time analyzing size of school as it relates to your particular likes and dislikes, your personality, your values, and your characteristics. The worst thing students can do is choose a school and find out they are unhappy with how they fit in. Peer pressure, especially at the freshmen level can be strong. Know yourself as best you can before you try to know colleges.

Step 3 – For those who wish to look deeper to create a short list of colleges, include additional preferences

If necessary, you can narrow down your list of colleges further by adding more filters on your search that screen for other important variables – perhaps even deal-breaker offerings or characteristics. Some of the more common factors include the following:

Graduation Rates

Presumably, your goal is to obtain a degree. Some colleges are much better at graduating students than others, but, as was pointed out earlier, some institutions admit extremely well prepared students who are more likely to succeed and, in the process, boost the college's four-year graduation rate. College's that enroll students with less rigorous college preparation do not experience the same benefit. *College Confidential College Search* and *U.S. Department of Education College Scorecard* provide easy access to individual college graduation rates. *The Chronicle of Higher Education College Completion* identifies the following 2010 highest and lowest six-year graduation rates. The site also provides four-year graduation figures.

Colleges with the Highest Six-Year Graduation Rates

1. Harvard University, Cambridge, MA (87.1%)
2. Yale University, New Haven, CT (88.9%)
3. University of Notre Dame, Notre Dame, IN (90.0%)
4. Princeton University, Princeton, NJ (90.1%)
5. Brown University, Providence, RI (85.7%)
6. University of Pennsylvania, Philadelphia, PA (88.6%)
7. Dartmouth College, Hanover, NH (88.1%)
8. Williams College, Williamstown, MA (91.0%)
9. Stanford University, Stanford, CA (78.4%)
10. Wesleyan University, Middletown, CT (89.1%)

Colleges with the Lowest Six-Year Graduation Rates

1. Vincennes University, Vincennes, IN (0.0%)
2. University of Phoenix Online, Phoenix, AZ (0.7%)
3. Western Governors University, Salt Lake City, UT (2.6%)
4. University of Houston, Houston, TX (1.0%)
5. International Academy of Design and Technology Chicago, Chicago, IL (8.9%)
6. Texas Southern University, Houston, TX (5.9%)
7. Cameron University, Lawton, OK (5.4%)
8. Utah Valley University, Orem, UT (3.9%)
9. University of Phoenix-Southern California Campus, Costa Mesa, CA (4.1%)
10. American InterContinental University, Atlanta, Georgia (12.8%)

Starting Salaries after Graduation - Return on Investment

As college costs skyrocket into the stratosphere, most students and parents are concerned about the salaries that will be earned after graduation relative to the huge bundle of money ponied up to earn a bachelor's degree. The *NerdScholar* and *CNN Money* sites report the schools with the highest average salaries upon graduation. *PayScale College Education ROI Rankings* presents a list of over 1,500 schools ranked according to their thirty-year return on investment (ROI) for a bachelor's degree. The site receives data from users who fill out questionnaires about their salaries in exchange for information that allows them to find out what a potential new job pays and/or whether they are currently earning a fair wage. *PayScale* has accumulated over forty million user-submitted profiles and, based on this data, the schools with the highest and lowest average starting salaries are listed as follows.

It must be pointed out that the academic major chosen by the student will greatly determine the starting salary.

Colleges with the Highest Average Starting Salaries

1. United States Naval Academy, Annapolis, MD ($77,100)
2. United States Military Academy at West Point, Highlands, NY ($74,000)
3. Harvey Mudd College, Claremont, CA ($73,300)
4. Massachusetts Institute of Technology, Cambridge, MA ($68,600)
5. California Institute of Technology, Pasadena, CA ($68,400)
6. Colorado School of Mines, Golden, CO ($66,700)
7. Rose-Hulman Institute of Technology, Terre Haute, IN ($65,100)
8. United States Air Force Academy, Air Force Academy, CO ($64,900)
9. Stevens Institute of Technology, Hoboken, NJ ($64,900)
10. Thomas Jefferson University, Philadelphia, PA ($64,400)

Colleges with the Lowest Average Starting Salaries

1. Coker College, Hartsville, SC ($29,700)
2. College of the Ozarks, Point Lookout, MO ($31,100)
3. Lee University, Cleveland, TN ($31,500)
4. University of Montevallo, Montevallo, AL ($31,500)
5. Wingate University, Wingate, NC ($31,600)
6. Central State University, Wilberforce, OH ($32,000)
7. University of Arkansas, Pine Bluff, AR ($32,000)
8. University of Phoenix, Omaha, NE ($32,100)
9. Wayne State College, Wayne, NE ($32,300)
10. Concord University, Athens, WV ($32,300)

Curriculum

If you have a major in mind, review the requirements for that major. Do the courses cover the areas you want to study? Students will attend a relatively small percentage of classes in their major, at least in the first year. Some curriculums allow students to sample a wide range of courses in different subjects while others are less flexible. It is important to know what courses are required to graduate, especially if you have significant issues with certain areas of study. A well-designed core curriculum gives students the broad base of knowledge they need to compete successfully in our globalized economy and to make sense of the modern world. Roper Public Affairs and Media firm found that some institutions do not require students to take any classes in basic economics, math, science, writing, and U.S. history before they graduate. *What Will They Learn?* is a useful site that ranks core academic requirements at all the major public and private universities in all 50 states. A sampling of those colleges receiving "A" and "F" grades are listed below:

Randomly Selected Colleges with "A" Grade Core Academic Requirements

Baylor University, Waco, TX
City University of New York - Brooklyn College, New York, NY
Gardner-Webb University, Boiling Springs, NC
Morehouse College, Atlanta, GA
Regent University, Virginia Beach, VA
St. John's College, Santa Fe, NM
Thomas More College of Liberal Arts, Merrimack, NH
United States Coast Guard Academy, New London, CT
University of Dallas, Irving, TX
University of Science and Arts of Oklahoma, Chickasha, OK

Randomly Selected Colleges with "F" Grade Core Academic Requirements

Alfred University, Alfred, NY
Capital University, Bexley, OH
DePauw University, Greencastle, IN
Grinnell College, Grinnell, IA
Kalamazoo College, Kalamazoo, MI
Pitzer College, Claremont, CA
St. John Fisher College, Rochester, NY
University of Colorado, Colorado Springs, CO
Walsh University, North Canton, OH

Whittier College, Whittier, CA

Median Borrowing

This figure represents the typical amount families borrow to fund a student's undergraduate studies. In 2012, average student loan debt was $28,720 upon graduation, according to a Hamilton Place Strategies study reported in the *The Huffington Post*. *The U.S. Department of Education College Scorecard* provides the total loan amount as well as the average monthly payment. Data presented by *College InSight* identifies the following schools which graduate students with low and high debt loads.

Four-Year Colleges with the Lowest Average Student Debt

1. CUNY York College, Jamaica, NY ($2,996)
2. California State University, Sacramento, CA ($3,541)
3. Clarion University of Pennsylvania, Clarion, PA ($3,815)
4. Elizabeth City State University, Elizabeth City, NC ($3,846)
5. Princeton University, Princeton, NJ ($5,330)
6. University of Houston-Clear Lake, Houston, TX ($6,726)
7. Dalton State College, Dalton, GA ($6,811)
8. College of the Ozarks, Point Lookout, MO ($7,062)
9. Pomona College, Claremont, CA ($7,540)
10. Berea College, Berea, KY ($7,661)

Four-Year Colleges with the Highest Average Student Debt

1. Lawrence Technological University, Southfield, MI ($46,677)
2. Johnson C. Smith University, Charlotte, NC ($46,673)
3. Wheelock College, Boston, MA ($45,391)
4. Delaware State University, Dover, DE ($45,098)
5. Franklin Pierce University, Rindge, NH ($44,702)
6. Sacred Heart University, Fairfield, CT ($44,538)
7. Widener University-Main Campus, Chester, PA ($44,430)
8. New England College, Henniker, NH ($43,808)
9. Salve Regina University, Newport, RI ($43,237)

10. Nova Southeastern University, Fort Lauderdale, FL ($43,201)

Loan Default Rate

This is the percentage of borrowers who defaulted on their federal student loans within three years of beginning repayment. It is an important statistic because it indicates the degree to which borrowers are unable to repay their loans, and the related ability to find employment after graduation. *U.S. Department of Education College Scorecard* provides loan default rate figures for individual institutions.

Freshmen Retention Rates

This represents the percentage of freshman who continue into their second academic year. It is an important measure because it verifies that students are on track to complete a degree in a timely manner. *College Confidential College Search* provides retention rates for individual colleges.

Sports and Activities

It is not unreasonable to consolidate your list of colleges by considering non-academic interests that include athletics, wellness activities, hobbies, and leadership opportunities. Nearly all four-year residential colleges offer a wide variety of sports, clubs and activities, but campuses do have very different characteristics. Some emphasize high profile sports while others highlight the performing arts, outdoor activities, intramural sports, volunteerism, personal fitness or Greek life. As mentioned above in the section of how you and the school might fit together, look for those schools that complement your interests. *College Confidential and College Board Big Future* provide search options for various sports, student organizations, and special interest groups.

Step 4 – Fine-tune your short list by reading online reviews, scanning brochures, visiting college websites and taking virtual tours

Visit the websites of those colleges on your short list and go to the admissions page to research additional information and take a virtual tour. Identify a suitable contact person who can answer any questions you may have, and find out if you could speak to a counselor who may be visiting in your area. If you like what you see, you may wish to sign up to receive follow-up communications from the school. This preliminary investigation will help you determine if you want to spend the time and money to visit the campus.

Be sure to scan through the various brochures you may have received, and recycle the ones that have piqued your interest. Student online comment sites, including *College Prowler* and *College Confidential*, offer student reflections and perspectives that may be worth reviewing. Consider joining the Facebook sites for your entering college class which will allow you to connect with other perspective students. Additional features you may wish to explore include:

Strong Career Services – guidance for landing an internship, job, and graduate study

Special Financial Aid Awards – colleges will provide monetary assistance if you qualify, and some are more generous than others

Academic Support Services – offers assistance when you are struggling with material you are learning

Internship Opportunities – hands-on, practical experiences look great on your resume

Travel Opportunities – international travel provides a global perspective valued by employers

Campus Safety – provides effective crime prevention services and a good safety record

Engaging Curriculum Features – logical, exciting and relevant course offerings

Student-faculty ratio – a lower ratio typically means more personal attention

Leadership Opportunities – an asset when applying for jobs or graduate programs

Average Class Size – large freshman lecture classes can be challenging for some students

High Quality Computing Infrastructure – provides the resources and bandwidth you'll need for academic work and personal enjoyment

Alumni Giving – the percentage of alums that donate may indicate how satisfied they are with their college experience

Strong Alumni Network – a powerful tool for mentoring, professional guidance and employment opportunities

Step 5 – Visit campuses and focus on at least a half dozen college finalists

Now you can physically visit each of the campuses on your short list to see the facilities and talk with faculty, staff and students. Break away from rehearsed, scripted tours and informally chat with students who are not trained by the Admissions team. Every college, like a family or local community, has its own culture with established values and traditions. You need to feel the campus vibes and atmosphere in order to determine if this is a place where you could comfortably fit in for the next four years. Is it a good fit for you? For a variety of reasons, some students find that a community college serves as a better alternative for the first two years rather than a more expensive four-year institution.

The bottom line is that there are many colleges that will be good for you. The most important thing is who you are and what you do with your time in the college you do attend. A few examples of successful individuals who attended non-famous colleges are Steve Jobs, Warren Buffet, Walt Disney, Tom Hanks, George Lucas, and Albert Einstein.

Step 6 – Apply for admission and financial aid

Now that you have boiled your list of potential college selections down to a manageable number of applications, it's time to proceed to the next chapter that will help you gain the maximum financial aid assistance. Only when the final awards are in can you determine which school will provide the most cost-effective, rewarding learning experience for you. As for financial aid, please do not linger. Remember: It's the early bird that gets the worm!

Tips for Landing the Best Financial Aid Deal

Most high school students are thinking about college in terms of academic program offerings, extracurricular activities, campus facilities and social atmosphere. But, when the financial aid packages arrive in the mail, decisions are made with costs in mind. Unfortunately, the aid award comes at the end of the search process.

Now and then a parent will ask us about the admissions process along with financial aid. Daniel was the most recent to ask. His daughter wanted to go to Yale, and if that were not possible, she had a fine backup school lined up. I asked him if he could pay the very expensive freight at Yale. It would be a struggle, but he would do whatever was needed. I asked him if his daughter had a good enough academic record to get into Yale. He thought it was border line, but he knew she would be most welcome by the backup school. He was shocked by my answer. He was a bit old school and was not up to date on what goes on behind the scenes. I told him to somehow let the people at Yale know he was able to pay for the full ride – no aid, no loans, no discounts, no scholarships. There are so few that can do this, causing the welcome mat to be a little bigger. If, on the other hand, she ends up planning to go to the backup school, then he should let them know that it is a bit tight, and he will definitely need aid. Because the backup school would relish having a really good student with high scores that will inflate the school's indices. They will find the resources to help out with a worthwhile discount.

The reality is that colleges are in a heated battle for a declining number of students. In this competitive market, some higher priced schools have been forced to dole out more money to help students pay for their huge charges. Even state schools are providing incentives to out-of-state students to make up for enrollment shortages. With this in mind, there are some simple steps you can take to ensure that your family will receive the best financial aid package possible. A slight twist on the old political election war cry becomes the golden rule of the entire financial aid process:

Apply early and apply often!

Step 1 – Complete the free application for federal aid (FAFSA)

This form should be submitted as soon as possible after January 1 of the year you are requesting aid. It's best to complete it online (http://www.fafsa.gov) since it reduces errors and speeds up the process. The schools you list on your FAFSA will have access to your data electronically within a day after it is processed. Keep in mind that failure to submit this form may disqualify you from receiving merit-based scholarships at some schools.

The FAFSA asks detailed questions about family income, investments savings, etc., and determines your eligibility for federal aid. The data is based on your tax return for the year before the student enrolls in college. The information you report on your FAFSA is used to calculate your expected family contribution (ECF). The schools you listed on your FAFSA will use your information to determine your eligibility for federal and institutional aid. Since the cost of attendance and aid policies differ from school to school, your aid eligibility and awards will vary among different institutions.

Many people aren't aware that the FAFSA form uses information from the family's tax returns for the previous year. Consequently, they don't initiate any strategies to adjust their incomes during that "base income year." As a parent considering what you are willing and able to pay, you should realize that the best way to save for college will also maximize your eligibility for financial aid. Knowing the rules about how aid is awarded will allow you to arrange your finances to reduce the amount of assets included in the formula that determines need. Some basic strategies:

> **If there's a chance you will be eligible for aid, don't put any money in your child's name, since federal formulas require that more of the student's money be used to defray college expenses. Typically for students, 20 percent of assets and 50 percent of income will be included in the calculation to determine how much they can pay, whereas parents are assessed 5.65 percent of assets and 47 percent of income. So, consider spending your child's**

assets rather than your own before submitting the FAFSA, or transfer those assets to a 529 Plan.

Consider 529 education savings accounts, which are treated as assets owned by the parent, even if they're in the student's name. These tax-advantaged investment vehicles were designed to encourage saving for the future higher education expenses of a child. There are two types of 529 plans: prepaid tuition plans and savings plans. Prepaid tuition plans allow for the pre-purchase of tuition based on today's rates and then paid out at the future cost when the beneficiary is in college. Savings plans are based on the market performance of the underlying investments, which typically consist of mutual funds, money market or other guaranteed options designed to protect an investor's principal.

If feasible, realistically minimize discretionary income during the base income year – the year before your child begins college. For example, avoid significant capital gains or the sale of property before January 1. Don't cash in savings bonds during that critical year and steer away from early retirement distributions.

Debt, in the form of a mortgage, car loan, credit cards, etc. does not decrease eligibility for financial aid, but cash does. Consider using a reasonable amount of accumulated liquid savings to pay down debt, or move up the schedule for planned future purchases.

Generally, pensions and retirement funds are not counted as assets when calculating financial aid eligibility. Contributing more in your 401(k) fund can not only boost your retirement savings, but also increase your odds for a larger aid award.

Step 2 – Complete required college aid applications as early as possible

In addition to the FAFSA, some colleges, but certainly not all, require their own financial aid form to help calculate the expected family contribution for each student. One such tool, the College Scholarship Service Profile (CSS) is used primarily by private institutions. The form gathers information about family incomes, liabilities, assets, veterans benefits, child support payments and so on.

Although the FAFSA doesn't ask about home ownership, the CSS does. Some institutions insist on knowing how much home equity you have accumulated, and factor that into their aid packaging formulas. Others do not. Read the financial aid rules before sending in the form, so your expectations will be realistic.

Most institutional student financial aid money is limited, and is frequently awarded on a first-come, first-served basis. Submitting your application early ensures that you'll be considered for the maximum amount of aid for which you qualify.

Step 3 – Search for scholarships

You may be surprised to find that a wide array of awards is available, even for those individuals who are neither high-performing nor high-need students. The best place to start is with the schools where you applied. Check out each college's website, catalog, and financial aid materials to find out what kinds of scholarships are available. Some awards are generally offered to all freshmen while others may be restricted to certain majors, talents or other characteristics. Many colleges will automatically consider you for one of its merit scholarships when you submit an admissions application or financial aid application.

As more students and their families question whether it is worth taking on massive amounts of debt just to end up with a dismal employment outlook, many private colleges are desperately offering all kinds of special discount deals for specific categories of students. For example, *The New York Times* reported that Seton Hall is offering two-thirds off the regular tuition sticker price for early applicants in the top 10% of their high school graduating class, a discount of some $21,000. TribLive reported that Duquesne University is intensifying its efforts to recruit students for its school of education and is offering a 50% discount on tuition and fees for all freshmen who enroll in the School of Education. Juniata College offers a 4-year graduation guarantee that covers the costs of any courses in a student's major that need to be taken after his or her fourth year, according to an article in *Forbes* titled, "Tuition Discount Alert: 50 Great Colleges Desperately Seeking Students."

You may also qualify for some local scholarships. Check with your guidance counselor or principal about awards for students graduating from your high school and for residents of your town, county and state. Explore personal and social affiliations such as Rotary International, Kiwanis, chamber of commerce, churches, area businesses, corporations, professional organizations and civic groups. Talk to your parents about possible scholarships that may be offered by their employers.

There are some amazing scholarships out there for students who have "experience with ghosts, telepathy and psychic powers," and others who demonstrate "marble shooter skills" or have a "strong interest in the future of the soybean industry," according to a great online scholarship search engine, *Fastweb.com*. Two other popular free online resources for finding scholarship cash are *Scholarships.com* and *CollegeBoard.com*.

Step 3 – Carefully review each financial aid award package

Financial aid officers are human and can make mistakes. If the numbers seem out of whack, check with the aid office to see if there was an error – perhaps in the expected family contribution calculation.

As you look at your aid award, be sure you understand the differences among the various types of awards. Grants and scholarships don't have to be paid back, but loans do. Some colleges practice "frontloading" by offering students more money the first year than they do in subsequent years, just to get them in the door. Certain grants may be awarded for only one year, while others are available throughout the student's entire college career. Many scholarships are tied to a minimum grade point average. Understanding these variables is important, since they significantly affect your future costs.

If only a subsidized Stafford Loan is offered, and you don't have enough aid to cover all of your expenses, you may want to ask about an unsubsidized Stafford Loan, a Perkins Loan or PLUS Loan. Another possibility some parents have is a home equity loan which may carry a lower interest rate than the Perkins or PLUS Loans. Stated simply, go for the loan with the lowest fixed interest rate, since variable rates may rise to higher levels during the years your child is paying it back. Consider using a home equity line of credit rather than an equity loan because the interest you pay will still be tax deductible, but you only pull down the amount of money you need. If you borrow excess money, it will be considered an asset and reduce your aid eligibility the following year.

If a Federal Work-Study Award is not included, you may not be eligible for one, or perhaps you didn't indicate an interest when you completed the FAFSA. You may want to ask about that. If you don't qualify for Work-Study, inquire about on-campus job opportunities. Research shows that students who work on campus develop stronger connections with faculty, staff, and students and tend to be more successful than those that don't. It would be especially beneficial to land a position in the academic department related to your major, since it may help with your studies and professional development.

Step 4 – Be prepared to appeal your financial aid award

The big secret in financial aid is that negotiating is widespread. In an *ABC News* article, Kal Chany, president of Campus Consultants Inc. and author of *Paying For College Without Going Broke*, offers this perspective:

> **The first aid package you get isn't necessarily the final offer and not necessarily the best offer from the school. You have more leverage than you think you do but you have to ask for it. Their view is, if we can get you to come to the school and only give you X amount of aid, why should we give you X plus when you're going to come anyway.**

Basically, if a college believes the student will attend only if a better award package is offered, the financial aid office may throw in some additional bucks. You have nothing to lose by tactfully requesting a reassessment. Consider the extra time and effort as an investment in your education. Along the way you may also enhance your self-advocacy skills, which may serve as an asset for you down the road.

But don't approach the process with the expectation that you are bargaining for a used car. School policies on negotiating aid awards vary greatly. Some actually encourage it, while others are inclined not to budge from their initial award. The student who received the award letter, not the parent, should initiate the appeal by writing a well-crafted letter to the author of the award letter, or otherwise the Director of Financial Aid. Some basic pointers:

First, always be courteous. Begin by thanking the school for its generous offer and describe why you are motivated to attend that particular college. If you bring any special skills, talents or characteristics that will enhance the campus atmosphere (choir singer, debater, theatrical performer, resident of a far away state, etc.) point that out. Then, present a convincing argument about why you'll need additional financial assistance to attend. You love the school and will be a positive campus influence, but you need to make it more affordable in order to enroll.

If the FAFSA formula indicates that you still have some unmet need, even after your financial aid award is applied, mention it.

If your family has financial burdens that weren't evident on the FAFSA form, such as medical expenses or extensive uninsured property damage, include documentation to verify the situation.

Keep in mind that if you are applying for admission into a struggling, low-enrollment major, as opposed to one with a waiting list, the college will be more

motivated to offer additional assistance.

Some colleges have a policy to match other schools' aid awards. Be sure to include copies of any larger aid packages you received from other institutions. If, after factoring in aid, the bottom line cost at the other schools is lower, the college will be especially inclined to sweeten the pot with some additional funding. If you're an outstanding student and have plenty of offers, you have a greater chance of receiving an upgraded financial award at your first-choice school.

If there has been a recent change in family circumstances that affects your financial situation, such as a job loss, health issues, sudden caretaking responsibilities, a dramatic plunge in the value of assets, etc., describe your new situation in detail.

Picture this. Sitting around a conference room table at a small private college is a Financial Aid Appeals Committee comprised of the Admissions Director, Financial Aid Director, a few professional counselors from both offices, and the Vice-President of Enrollment Management. Up for consideration of her award appeal is Joyce, an in-state prospective business management major. Her letter states that she is impressed by the school, friendly campus, the Business Department, and the wonderful state-of-the-art facilities. She goes on to state that this college is her top choice, but finances are a concern. Joyce reveals that she was accepted at five other colleges and received larger scholarship awards from two of them. Copies of those awards were attached to the letter of appeal.

The Director of Admission retrieves Joyce's high school record. The report shows that the student has a slightly-above-average 3.2 grade point average with similar SAT scores and high school class rank. The Director then points out that the number of business management majors is strong, but there is still plenty of room.

The Financial Aid Director views his computer screen and indicates that, after all the aid awards have been applied, Joyce still has an unmet need of $4,300. Yes, she sent her FAFSA results to five other schools, noted on the FAFSA site, which he precedes to name. Three are state schools that probably didn't offer much financial assistance. Looking at the two much more expensive colleges that provided larger aid packages, the Director does some quick calculations. When the aid amounts from both private schools are subtracted from their much higher costs of attendance, the out-of-pocket expenses are still $8,000 to 11,500 higher than this college. In other words, the net difference cost is significantly greater at both of those private institutions as compared to the appeal college. However, the net difference between the three state universities and the appeal college ranges from $5,500 to $8,200 lower.

The Enrollment Management VP summarizes by saying that it doesn't make much sense to offer Joyce more aid based on the award packages given by the two private schools, since net costs at those institutions are already significantly higher. And, it is impractical to try to match the state university pricing. It is assumed that the value-added quality features of a private education will justify the added expenses. If not, there is simply no way to compete against the state system solely on the basis of cost.

The Committee discusses its options. Joyce is a relatively good student and there is ample space in the business management major. She still has some unmet need and may consider a state school option if funds are an issue. The Committee decides to offer Joyce a Work-Study position of $1,500 to help defray expenses and close the need gap. They hope it will be enough of an added incentive to move her away from the state schools.

What have we learned here? Institutions are sometimes willing to adjust their aid packages depending on available funds, a family's financial need, and offers from the competition that include a lower net price. It also depends on how much the school wants a particular student. High performing students will garner more money. So will students with special talents or desirable backgrounds, as well as those who are pursuing majors that need an enrollment boost.

Step 5 – Compare and decide

After the financial aid packages from your short list colleges have arrived, it's time to prioritize the options. Let's assume you were accepted to seven institutions and received a financial aid award package from all of them. For each college, calculate the net out-of-pocket expenses you'll need to pay by subtracting the total grants and scholarships (not loans, since they must be repaid) from the cost of attendance. Then, rank the list of seven colleges from lowest net cost to highest.

If, as a result of your college search parameters, the institutions are essentially in the same ballpark relative to most other important variables, you have just created your very own best bang for the buck college list. But, it's never really quite that simple. There are usually other factors that may make it worth your while to pay the additional expense. Will the same amount of aid money be available during the upperclass years, or is some of the grant money provided only to freshman? If you love horses and one of the institutions offers an outstanding equestrian program, you may be willing to fork over more tuition dollars for the experience. Maybe you feel strongly about the new state-of-the-art Nursing facilities coupled with strong employment opportunities at a school that costs a bit more. These are personal decisions that only you can make.

In summary, we know that going to college is an expensive proposition, much more so than it was years ago. Every student and parent should try to reduce the cost through all the avenues mentioned in this chapter. This would include scholarships both large and small (and there are many), well-understood loans (here again, there are a variety to consider), and discounts which often pass as scholarships. Finally, there is the power of negotiations which is a relatively new ingredient in the college selection process. Do not be afraid to try it. Let one school know what another school is willing to do for you relative to financial matters.

Postscript 1 – Change

Change: the concept that frightens the old, but excites the young. Students sometimes want it just to show their mettle. Professors often do not want it because it may move them from a comfort zone in which they have become accustomed. However, change must receive its due.

Consider the enormous change that has occurred over the years in the field of medicine; not only its application, but its delivery. Of course technology and discovery have been a tremendous impetus in its continued change and growth. But its delivery has changed dramatically also. Not so long ago the doctor was addressing many, if not all, sorts of ailments. And he (very few she's) worked alone and made house calls. Then there were groups of doctors working in group practices, and specialties were growing. More recently doctors became employees of the hospitals, which in turn grew in size and merged with other hospitals, the better to negotiate with the large insurance companies. All of this, and more, in one person's lifetime.

Consider manufacturing. From essentially handmade to production lines, including robots, to methods and specifications that boggle the mind – mainly of older folk. Most of these changes occurred in a person's lifetime.

Consider the military. From tactics and equipment that focused mainly on numbers of personal, along with primitive weapons, all the way through nuclear arms to unmanned drones. Even now, the strategy is to not remain static. Just about all these changes occurred in a person's life time.

Consider the flow of information media. Perhaps no endeavor has changed as much and as fast as this endeavor. Books and newspapers were with us for centuries. The radio much less so. And TV much more recently. The delivery of TV has exploded in every which way. The older people resist the change simply because they cannot keep up with it – including the complexities of the remote! The young people welcome the changes simply because they are very dexterous with their fingers and their minds. Books remain books, but their delivery has changed to include the Internet. Newspapers have fallen victim to the Internet, with many weakened or depleted. They have either changed too slowly or not at all. And just about all the vivid change in information flow has occurred in a person's lifetime.

Changes do occur at the college level, but in most cases they are likened to pulling up an intransigent deeply rooted weed. Faculty committees mull over the proposed change forever. Deans and presidents are tentative and fear unwelcome repercussions. Boards of trustees are not forceful enough in getting answers that differ from the status quo. On this point, the overwhelming majority of Board members are themselves college graduates of a bygone era who think things should be as they were when they were in college. They, as with many professors and college administrators, like the stability and tradition of the place. As president, I was explaining to the trustees an incident in the dormitory that made some headlines. One trustee asked if dorm mothers did not instruct the boys, and discipline them, if they got out of line – as they did when he was in college. He was a very successful businessman. I replied that if he ran his business the way it was run 50 years ago, he might not be as successful as he is today. He understood immediately that changes had occurred in living accommodations throughout the country.

Other changes in college life have to occur. This book has focused mainly on finances. College costs are out of control, and we have given the reasons why, and the solutions needed. Other changes, big changes, need to be considered to address both the delivery methods and the composition of the student body. No endeavor can survive only on the successes of the past. This is not to say the study of history, or philosophy, or other traditional courses has to change. The delivery, and to whom it is being delivered needs review. Just as the packaging of a complete degree needs review. College personnel at every level need to reconsider their views and response to those families and students that have reasonable expectations of a job after four or more years of college life accompanied by large payments and extended loans.

It might be appropriate to close with Di Lampedusa's admonition:

If you want things to stay the same, then we will have to make some changes.

Postscript 2 – A Cost/Income System

Any cost/system, to be effective, must be understood by as many professors as possible, including those who teach in fields far removed from numbers. The more professors understand it, the more they will buy into it.

This cost/income system starts with the individual professor. It takes one class and assigns the college tuition rate to each student regardless of whether or not the student paid the full rate, is on partial scholarship, or on full scholarship. Using an example where the numbers are easy, suppose the tuition is $30,000 per year. The student takes 15 credits per semester, so each three-credit class costs $3,000. Thus, a professor teaching such a class is considered to have contributed $3,000 for every student in this class. If there are 25 students, then he is credited with 25 times $3,000, or a total of $75,000. If he teaches four classes with 25, 20, 15, and 20 students, he is credited with a total of $3,000 times 80 or $240,000.

His cost would be his salary for the year, which for ease of example, we'll set at $100,000. Thus his cost/income would be 100,000/240,000, which turns out to be 41%. Each professor in this department has a cost/income, as does the entire department. It is not difficult to do a five year retrospective of the department, thereby establishing an historical cost/income for this particular department. For the sake of this example, let us say it turns out to be 41%. The dean and the chairperson sit down and discuss a future cost/income as a goal, let us say 40%. With that as a goal, the chairperson can run courses as she sees fit….provided it comes in at or below 40%. Experience tells us that chemistry departments will have a higher cost/income than business courses. While every department may differ one from the other, the entire college is the aggregate of all the departments.

Each college or university may have a different cost/income; remember, the five-year historical perspective will set the bar from which to begin negotiations. At the college where both authors worked, we had a 40% faculty cost/income once all departments were amalgamated.

Of course, the faculty wanted to know how the administration was being judged regarding cost/income. Without going into detail, it was satisfactorily developed and shared with everyone. After a few years, most were comfortable with it. Not only did it control cost, it provided each department with more authority to run under-enrolled classes so long as it did not drag down their particular cost/income ratio. I should add that for every college there will be some customizing, but it should be emphasized that the process must be understood by a vast majority of the faculty. With each added complexity, understanding by some faculty members will be lost, as will be trust in the system. Also, including the administration in a comparable cost/income system is equally important to secure the critical trust of the faculty as well as to reduce the size and cost of the non-teaching staff.

References

Preface

G.D. Di Lampedusa, *The Leopard: A Novel* (New York: *Pantheon*, 2007).

Chapter 1

J.S. Brubaker and W. Rudy, *Higher Education in Transition: A History of American Colleges, 1636–1976, Higher Education in Transition* (New York: Harper & Row, 1976).

Hearing before the Select House Committee on Children, Youth, and Families, "College Education: Paying More and Getting Less" (Washington, DC: U.S. Government Printing Office, 1992).

Hearing before the House Subcommittee on Education and Labor, "Higher Education Costs" (Washington, DC: U.S. Government Printing Office, 1987).

R.V. Iosue, "Who Pays for the High Costs of Low Tuition?" *Newsday,* October 26, 1975.

R.V. Iosue, "How Colleges Can Cut Costs," *Wall Street Journal,* January 27, 1987.

Oversight Hearing on the Reauthorization of the Higher Education Act of 1965, (Washington, DC: U.S. Government Printing Office, 1985).

Chapter 2

R.C. Dickeson, "Frequently Asked Questions About College Costs," Sixth in a series of Issue Papers released by The Secretary of Education's Commission on the Future of Higher Education, 2006, http://www.csupomona.edu/~rosenkrantz/prpc/costsdickeson.pdf.

S. Hurtado, K. Eagan, J.H. Pryor, H. Whang, and S. Tran, "Undergraduate Teaching Faculty: The 2010–11 HERI Faculty Survey," Higher Education Research Institute, University of California, Los Angeles, 2012, http://www.heri.ucla.edu/monographs/HERI-FAC2011-Monograph.pdf.

J. E. Morley Jr., "Explaining College Costs," National Association of College and University Business Officers, February, 2002, http://www.nacubo.org/Research/NACUBO_Research_Projects/College_Pricing_and_Financial_Aid/Cost_of_College_Study.html.

Chapter 3

D.M. Desrochers and R. Kirshstein, "Labor Intensive or Labor Expensive: Changing Staffing and Compensation Patterns in Higher Education," The Delta Cost Project at American Institutes for Research, February, 2014, http://www.deltacostproject.org/sites/default/files/products/DeltaCostAIR_Staffing_Brief_2_3_14.pdf.

J.P. Green, "Administrative Bloat at American Universities: The Real Reason for High Costs in Higher Education," The Goldwater Institute, 2010, http://goldwaterinstitute.org/sites/default/files/Administrative%20Bloat.pdf.

S. Lipka, "Federal Probe of Sexual Assault at U. of Montana Yields 'Blueprint for Colleges,'" *The Chronicle of Higher Education*, May 10, 2013, http://chronicle.com/article/Federal-Investigation-of/139177/.

Chapter 5

S. Cohn, "Student Loan Debt Hits Record High, Study Shows," Business, NBCNews.com, October 18, 2012, http://www.nbcnews.com/business/student-loan-debt-hits-record-high-study-shows-1C6542975.

J. Delisle, "The Graduate Student Debt Review," New America Education Policy Program, March, 2014, http://newamerica.net/sites/newamerica.net/files/policydocs/GradStudentDebtReview-Delisle-Final.pdf.

R. Fry, "A Record One-in-Five Households Now Owe Student Loan Debt," Pew Research Social & Demographic Trends, Pew Research Center, September 26, 2012, http://www.pewsocialtrends.org/2012/09/26/a-record-one-in-five-households-now-owe-student-loan-debt/.

"How America Pays for College," Sallie Mae and Ipsos, Sallie Mae Inc., 2012, https://www1.salliemae.com/NR/rdonlyres/75C6F178-9B25-48F5-8982-41F9B3F35BF6/0/HowAmericaPays2012.pdf.

"Job Openings and Labor Turnover Summary," U.S. Bureau of Labor Statistics, February 12, 2013, www.bls.go.

M. Kantrowitz, "Student Loan Debt Clock," *FinAid Page LLC*, 2013, http://www.finaid.org/loans/studentloandebtclock.phtml.

M. Kantrowitz, "Tuition Inflation," *FinAid Page LLC*, 2013, http://www.finaid.org/savings/tuition-inflation.phtml.

J. Leo, "Janitors with College Degrees and the Higher-Education Bubble," *The Newsweek/Daily Beast Company LLC*, July 18, 2012, http://www.thedailybeast.com/articles/2012/07/18/janitors-with-college-degrees-and-the-higher-education-bubble.html.

"Quarterly Report on Household Debt and Credit," Federal Reserve Bank of New York, Q3, 2012, http://www.newyorkfed.org/householdcredit/.

M. Reed and D. Cochrane, "Student Debt and the Class of 2012," The Institute for College Access & Success (TICAS), December, 2013, http://www.ticas.org/pub_view.php?idx=922.

J. Sanburn, "Higher-Education Poll," *TIME,* October 18, 2012, http://

nation.time.com/2012/10/18/higher-education-poll/.

J. Selingo, "Fixing College," Opinion Pages, *New York Times*, June 25, 2012, http://www.nytimes.com/2012/06/26/opinion/fixing-college-through-lower-costs-and-better-technology.html.

M. Stratford, "Grad Student Debt Rising," *Inside Higher Ed*, March 25, 2014, http://www.insidehighered.com/news/2014/03/25/new-america-report-provides-snapshot-rising-debt-burdens-graduate-students.

C. Stone, C.V. Horn, and C. Zukin, "Chasing the American Dream: Recent College Graduates and the Great Recession," Rutgers, The State University of New Jersey, May 2012, http://www.heldrich.rutgers.edu/sites/default/files/content/Chasing_American_Dream_Report.pdf.

"Total Fall Enrollment in Degree-granting Institutions, by Attendance Status, Sex, and Age: Selected Years, 1970 Through 2020," Institute of Education Sciences National Center for Education Statistics, U.S. Department of Education, 2011, http://nces.ed.gov/programs/digest/d11/tables/dt11_200.asp.

H. Yen, M. Valdes, T. Loller, C. Silva, and S. Chereb, "Half of Recent College Grads Underemployed or Jobless, Analysis Says," *Associated Press*, April 23, 2012, http://www.cleveland.com/business/index.ssf/2012/04/half_of_recent_college_grads_u.html.

Chapter 6

"A Brief History of Overlap and the Antitrust Suit," *MIT News*, September 3, 1992, http://web.mit.edu/newsoffice/1992/history-0903.html.

Kari Andren, "Duquesne to Cut Tuition, Fees in Half for New Education Majors," TribLive News, August 7, 2011, http://triblive.com/x/pittsburghtrib/news/breaking/s_752007.html#axzz2Vp87B5sb.

S. Baum, L. Lapovsky, and J. Ma, "Tuition Discounting: Institutional Aid Patterns at Public and Private Colleges and Universities, 2000–2001 to 2008–09," The College Board Advocacy & Policy Center, The College Board, September, 2010, http://advocacy.collegeboard.org/sites/default/files/10b_1976_TuitionDiscountReport_Int_WEB_100910.pdf.

S. Baum and J. Ma, "2012, Trends in College Pricing," College Board Advocacy & Policy Center, The College Board, http://advocacy.collegeboard.org/sites/default/files/college-pricing-2012-full-report_0.pdf.

E. Hoover and J. Keller, "More Students Migrate Away From Home," *The Chronicle of Higher Education,* October 30, 2011, http://chronicle.com/article/The-Cross-Country-Recruitment/129577/.

Sallie Mae, Inc., "How America Pays for College 2012, Sallie Mae's National Study of College Students and Parents," conducted by Ipsos Public Affairs, 2012, https://www1.salliemae.com/NR/rdonlyres/75C6F178-9B25-48F5-8982-41F9B3F35BF6/0/HowAmericaPays2012.pdf.

S. Jaschik and D. Lederman, "Perspectives on the Downturn: A Survey of Presidents," *Inside Higher Ed,* March 4, 2011, http://www.insidehighered.com/news/survey/president2011.

K. Kiley, "Short-Term Focus, Long-Term Problems: A Survey of Business Officers," *Inside Higher Ed*, July, 2012, http://www.insidehighered.com/news/survey/business_officer_2012.

D. Lederman, D., "Baby Steps for Need-Based Aid," *Inside Higher Ed*, January 7, 2013, http://www.insidehighered.com/news/2013/01/07/private-college-presidents-push-campaign-limit-use-non-need-based-aid.

New Georgia Encyclopedia, s.v. "Hope Scholarship," http://www.georgiaencyclopedia.org.

R. Pérez-Peña, "College Offers Top Applicants Two-Thirds Off," *New York Times*, September 28, 2011, http://www.nytimes. com/2011/09/29/nyregion/seton-hall-university-to-offer-steep-tuition-discounts.html.

N. Pullaro, "2011 Survey of Tuition Discounting Study Report, National Association of College and University Business Officers, 2012, http://www.nacubo.org/Research/Research_News/2011_NACUBO _Tuition_Discounting_Study_Released.html.

M. Reed, and R. Shireman, "Time to Re-examine Institutional Cooperation on Financial Aid," Institute for College Access and Success, June, 2008, http://www.ticas.org/files/pub/antitrust.pdf.

D. Troop, "Near-Term Outlook Is Bleak for All of Higher Education, Moody's Says," *The Chronicle of Higher Education,* January 6, 2013, http://chronicle.com/blogs/bottomline/near-term-outlook-is-bleak-for-all-of-higher-education-moodys-says/.

"Tuition Freeze & Four-Year Guarantee," *Burlington College*, accessed February 10, 2013, https://www.burlington.edu/.

Chapter 7

A. P. Carnevale, B. Cheah, and J. Strohl, "Hard Times, Georgetown University Center on Education and the Workforce," *Georgetown University*, January 4, 2012, http://cew.georgetown.edu/ unemployment/.

C. Condon and P. Weisman, "Manufacturers Cutting White-Collar Jobs Now, Too," *Daily Tribune* (Clinton Township, MI), January 24, 2013, http://www.dailytribune.com/article/20130124/ FINANCE01/130129744/manufacturers-cutting-white-collar-jobs-now-too.

"Consumer Price Index," Division of Consumer Prices and Price Indexes, U.S. Bureau of Labor Statistics, January 16, 2013, http:// www.bls.gov.

B. Covert, "Recession Has Lit the Fuse on Explosive Student Debt, Next New Deal," The Blog of the Roosevelt Institute, n.d., http://www.nextnewdeal.net/recession-has-lit-fuse-explosive-student-debt.

C. Fletcher, "A Message to Aspiring Lawyers: Caveat Emptor," *Wall Street Journal,* January 2, 2013, http://online.wsj.com/article/SB100 01424127887323320404578213223967518096.html.

R. Haskins, "Combating Poverty: Understanding New Challenges for Families," Social Genome Project Research Number 38, United States Senate Committee on Finance, June 5, 2012, http://www.brookings.edu/research/testimony/2012/06/05-poverty-families-haskins.

H. Johnson, "Defunding Higher Education. What Are the Effects on College Enrollment?" Public Policy Institute of California, May 2012, http://www.ppic.org/content/pubs/report/R_512HJR.pdf.

D. Kadlec, "Here We Go Again: Is College Worth It?" Business and Money, *Time*, April 17, 2012, http://business.time.com/2012/04/17/here-we-go-again-is-college-worth-it/.

T. Kalwarski, D. Mosher, J. Paskin, and D. Rosato, "Best Jobs in America: *MONEY Magazine* and Salary.com Rate Careers on Salary and Job Prospects." Cable News Network, 2006, http://money.cnn.com/magazines/moneymag/bestjobs/2006/.

K. Kensing, "The 10 Least Stressful Jobs of 2013," *Career Cast*, 2013, http://www.careercast.com/jobs-rated/10-least-stressful-jobs-2013.

J. Marcus, "College Enrollment Shows Signs of Slowing," *Hechinger Report*, May 31, 2012, http://hechingerreport.org/content/college-enrollment-shows-signs-of-slowing_8688/.

S. Peters, "MOOCs Approved for Credit, But Who Cares?" *Enterprise Efficiency*, February 16, 2013, http://www.enterpriseefficiency.com/

author.asp?section_id=1134&doc_id=259041.

J. H. Pryor, M.K. Eagan, L.P. Blake, S. Hurado, J. Berdan, and M.H. Case, "Survey: More Freshmen Than Ever Say They Go to College to Get Better Jobs, Make More Money," *The American Freshman: National Norms Fall 2012,* The Higher Education Research Institute, 2013, http://www.heri.ucla.edu/pr-display.php?prQry=111.

C. Rampell, "It Takes a B.A. to Find a Job as a File Clerk," *New York Times*, February 19, 2013, http://www.nytimes.com/2013/02/20/business/college-degree-required-by-increasing-number-of-companies.html?pagewanted=all&_r=0.

H. Shierholz, "New College Grads Losing Ground on Wages," Economic Policy Institute, August 31, 2011, http://www.epi.org/publication/new_college_grads_losing_ground_on_wages/.

D. Segal, D., "For 2nd Year, a Sharp Drop in Law School Entrance Tests," *New York Times,* March 19, 2012, http://www.nytimes.com/2012/03/20/business/for-lsat-sharp-drop-in-popularity-for-second-year.html.

P. Taylor, R. Fry, D. Cohn, W. Wang, G. Velasco, and D. Dockterman, "Is College Worth It?," Social & Demographic Trends, Pew Research Center, May 16, 2011, http://online.wsj.com/public/resources/documents/HigherEdReport.pdf.

R. Vedder, C. Denhart, and J. Robe, "Why Are Recent College Graduates Underemployed? University Enrollments and Labor-Market Realities, A Policy Paper from the Center for College Affordability and Productivity," January 2013, http://centerforcollegeaffordability.org/uploads/Underemployed%20Report%202.pdf.

R. Vedder, A. Gillen, D. Bennett, M. Denhart, J. Robe, T. Holbrook, P. Neiger, J. Coleman, J. Templeton, J. Leirer, L. Myers, R. Brady, and M. Malesick, "25 Ways to Reduce the Cost of College," Center for College Affordability and Productivity, 2010, http://

centerforcollegeaffordability.org/uploads/25Ways_to_Reduce_the_Cost_of_College.pdf.

D. Yankelovich, "College Presidents Are Too Complacent," *The Chronicle of Higher Education*, May 15, 2011, http://chronicle.com/article/College-Presidents-Are-Too/127529/.

H. Yen, C. Silva, and S. Chereb, "Half of Recent College Grads Underemployed or Jobless, Analysis Says," *Associated Press*, April 23, 2012, http://www.cleveland.com/business/index.ssf/2012/04/half_of_recent_college_grads_u.html.

Chapter 8

P. Abramson, "Slow and Steady," 19th Annual College Construction Report, *College Planning & Management,* February, 2014, http://webcpm.com/research/2014/02/college-construction-report/asset.aspx?tc=assetpg.

R. B. Archibald and D.H. Feldman, "The Real Cost Equation," *Inside Higher Ed*, October 19, 2010, http://www.insidehighered.com/views/2010/10/19/feldman.

D. Belkin, and S. Thurm, "Deans List: Hiring Spree Fattens College Bureaucracy – and Tuition," *Wall Street Journal*, December 28, 2012, http://online.wsj.com/article/SB10001424127887323316804578161490716042814.html.

K. Bromery, "Florida State Announces Plan to Continue to Rise in the National Rankings," *Florida State University*, February 5, 2013, http://news.fsu.edu/More-FSU-News/Florida-State-announces-plan-to-continue-rise-in-national-rankings.

"Despite Massive Budget Cuts, There's a Building Boom in U.S. Higher Education," *Hechinger Report*, National Association of Independent Colleges and Universities, April 2, 2012, http://www.naicu.edu/news_room/news_detail.asp?id=14211.

D. M. Desrochers, "Academic Spending Versus Athletic Spending: Who Wins?" Delta Cost Project at American Institutes for Research, 2012, http://www.deltacostproject.org/pdfs/DeltaCostAIR_Athletic Academic_Spending_IssueBrief.pdf.

R. C. Dickeson, "Frequently Asked Questions About College Costs," Sixth in a series of Issue Papers released by The Secretary of Education's Commission on the Future of Higher Education, 2006, http://www.csupomona.edu/~rosenkrantz/prpc/costsdickeson.pdf.

S. Dillon, "Share of College Spending for Recreation Is Rising," *New York Times*, July 9, 2010, http://www.nytimes.com/2010/07/10/ education/10education.html.

"Education Expenditures by Country," Institute of Education Sciences, National Center for Education Statistics, U.S. Department of Education, 2012, http://nces.ed.gov/programs/coe/indicator_ cmd.asp.

M. Finnegan and G. Holland, "Waste Throws Wrench Into Los Angeles Community Colleges' Massive Project," *Los Angeles Times*, February 27, 2011, http://articles.latimes.com/2011/feb/27/ local/la-me-build1-20110227.

R. H. Frank and P.J. Cook, *The Winner-Take-All Society: Why the Few at the Top Get So Much More Than the Rest of Us* (New York: Penguin Books, 1996).

J. P. Greene, "Administrative Bloat at American Universities: The Real Reason for High Costs in Higher Education," The Goldwater Institute, 2010, http://goldwaterinstitute.org/sites/default/files/ Administrative%20Bloat.pdf.

"Higher Education Spending & Performance," Policy Points by Commonwealth Foundation, April 6, 2011, http://www. commonwealthfoundation.org/issues/detail/higher-education- spending-performance.

B. Jacob, B. McCall, and K.M. Strange, "College as Country Club: Do Colleges Cater to Students' Preferences for Consumption?" National Bureau of Economic Research, January 2013, http://www. nber.org/papers/w18745.

S. Jaschik, "The Customer Is Always Right?" *Inside Higher Ed*, January 29, 2013, http://www.insidehighered.com/news/2013/01/29/ many-students-opt-colleges-spend-more-nonacademic-functions-study-finds.

A. Martin, "Building a Showcase Campus, Using An I.O.U.," *New York Times*, December 13, 2012, http://www.nytimes.com/2012/12/14/ business/colleges-debt-falls-on-students-after-construction-binges. html?pagewanted=all.

R. E. Martin and C.R. Hill, "Measuring Baumol and Bowen Effects in Public Research Universities," Social Science Electronic Publishing Inc., January 30, 2013, http://papers.ssrn.com/sol3/papers. cfm?abstract_id=2153122.

L. Olson and J. Crompton, "Cal U President's Firing, Release of Audit Report Stun Campus," *Pittsburgh Post-Gazette*, May 18, 2012, http://www.post-gazette.com/stories/news/education/armenti-firing-audit-stun-cal-u-636464/.

M. Whitaker, "A Ten-Year Perspective: California Infrastructure Spending, Legislative Analyst's Office," The California Legislature's Nonpartisan Fiscal and Policy Advisor, August 25, 2011, http:// www.lao.ca.gov/reports/2011/stadm/infrastructure/infrastructure _082511.aspx.

J. Woronkowicz, C. Joynes, N. Bradburn, R. Gertner, P. Frumkin, A. Kolendo, and B. Seaman, "Set in Stone, Building America's New Generation of Arts Facilities, 1994–2008," *University of Chicago*, 2012, http://culturalpolicy.uchicago.edu/setinstone/.

Chapter 9

M. Corkery, "Colleges Lose Pricing Power," *Wall Street Journal* online, http://online.wsj.com/article/SB10001424127887324442304 578231922159602676.html.

D. M. Desroches, C.M. Lentham, and J.V. Wellman, "Trends in College Spending 1998–2008," Delta Project on Postsecondary Education Costs, Productivity, and Accountability, 2010, http:// www.deltacostproject.org/resources/pdf/Trends-in-College-Spending-98-08.pdf.

S. Dillon, "Share of College Spending for Recreation Is Rising," *New York Times*, July 9, 2010, http://www.nytimes.com/2010/07/10/ education/10education.html.

R. Fry and M.H. Lopez, "Hispanic Student Enrollments Reach New Highs in 2011," Pew Research Center, August 20, 2012, http://www. pewhispanic.org/2012/08/20/hispanic-student-enrollments-reach-new-highs-in-2011/.

E. Hoover, "Why Counting Applications Is an Iffy Exercise," *The Chronicle of Higher Education*, September 24, 2013, http:// chronicle.com/blogs/headcount/counting-applications-is-an-iffy-exercise/36795?cid=at&utm_source=at&utm_medium=en.

"Immediate Transition to College, Graduation Rates, Institute of Education Sciences," National Center for Education Statistics, U.S. Department of Education, 2012, http://nces.ed.gov/fastfacts/display. asp?id=51.

"Income, Expenses, Poverty and Wealth," *Statistical Abstract of the United States: 2012,* U.S. Census Bureau, 2012, http://www. census.gov/compendia/statab/cats/income_expenditures_poverty_ wealth.html.

"Knocking at the Door, Projections of High school Graduates," Western Interstate Commission for Higher Education, December

2012, http://www.wiche.edu/pub/16556.

A. Martin, "Downturn Still Squeezes Colleges and Universities," *New York Times,* January 10, 2013, http://www.nytimes.com/2013/01/11/business/colleges-expect-lower-enrollment.html?_r=0.

S. Murray, "Grads Head to College in Record Numbers," *Wall Street Journal*, April 28, 2010, http://online.wsj.com/article/SB10001424052748703832204575210244203411342.html.

H. E. Nasser, "The Changing Faces of America, *USA Weekend*, January 18–20, 2013, http://www.usaweekend.com/apps/pbcs.dll/article?AID–2013301180005.

T. D. Snyder, S.A. Dillow, and C.A. Hoffman, "Digest of Educational Statistics," National Center for Educational Statistics, August 2007, http://nces.ed.gov/programs/digest/.

Chapter 10

K. Clark, "Colleges Play the Name Game," *U.S. News & World Report,* September 17, 2009, http://www.usnews.com/education/articles/2009/09/17/colleges-play-the-name-game?page=2.

P. D. McClusky, "'University' Is the Name of Choice for Many Colleges," *telegram.com,* June 24, 2013, http://www.telegram.com/article/20130602/NEWS/306029982/1002.

Chapter 11

K. Auletta, "Get Rich U.," *The New Yorker*, April 30, 2012, http://www.newyorker.com/reporting/2012/04/30/120430fa_fact_auletta.

T. Carmody,"'What's Wrong With Education Cannot Be Fixed with Technology' — The Other Steve Jobs," *Wired*, January 17, 2012, http://www.wired.com/business/2012/01/apple-education-jobs/.

A. Diaz, "College textbooks may become free at the University of Maryland," Liberty Voice, *University Business*, March 25, 2014, http://www.universitybusiness.com/news/college-textbooks-may-become-free-university-maryland.

G. A. Fowler, "An Early Report Card on Massive Open Online Courses," *Wall Street Journal*, October 8, 2013, http://online.wsj.com/news/articles/SB10001424052702303759604579093400834738972.

N. Harden, "The End of the University as We Know It," *The American Interest*, December 11, 2012, http://www.the-american-interest.com/articles/2012/12/11/the-end-of-the-university-as-we-know-it/.

J. Lane and K. Kinser, "MOOC's and the McDonaldization of Global Higher Education," *The Chronicle of Higher Education*, September 28, 2012, http://chronicle.com/blogs/worldwise/moocs-mass-education-and-the-mcdonaldization-of-higher-education/30536.

S. Kolowich, "New U. of California President Plays Down Online Education," *The Chronicle of Higher Education*, March 27, 2014, http://chronicle.com/blogs/wiredcampus/new-u-of-california-president-plays-down-online-education/51409.

L. Lang, "2013 Core Data Service Executive Summary Report," EDUCAUSE Center for Analysis and Research, February, 2014, http://www.educause.edu/library/resources/2013-cds-executive-summary-report.

D. Perez-Hernandez, "Taking Notes by Hand Benefits Recall, Researchers Find," *The Chronicle Of Higher Education*, March 27, 2014, http://chronicle.com/blogs/wiredcampus/taking-notes-by-hand-benefits-recall-researchers-find/51411.

L. Pappano, "The Year of the MOOC," *New York Times*, November 2, 2012, http://www.nytimes.com/2012/11/04/education/edlife/massive-open-online-courses-are-multiplying-at-a-rapid-pace.html?pagewanted=all.

P. Saettler, *A History of Instructional Technology* (New York: McGraw-Hill, 1968).

M. Stephens, "When Modifications Are a Must," *Business Officer*, July/August, 2012, http://www.nacubo.org/Business_Officer_Magazine/Magazine_Archives/JulyAugust_2012/Some_Great_Minds/When_Modifications_Are_a_Must.html.

Chapter 15

"AffordableCollegesOnline," *AffordableCollegesOnline*, 2013, http://www.affordablecollegesonline.org/.

D. Berrell, "Adjuncts Are Better Teachers Than Tenured Professors, Study Finds," *The Chronicle of Higher Education*, September 9, 2013, http://chronicle.com/article/Ad-juncts-Are-Bet-ter/141523/.

"The Chronicle of Higher Education's College Completion," *The Chronicle of Higher Education*, http://collegecompletion.chronicle.com/table/.

S. Adams, "The 25 Colleges With The Worst Return On Investment," *Forbes.com LLC*, 2013, http://www.forbes.com/sites/susanadams/2013/08/09/the-25-colleges-with-the-worst-return-on-investment/2/.

S. Adams, "25 Colleges With the Best Return on Investment," *Forbes.com LLC*, 2013, http://www.forbes.com/sites/susanadams/2013/05/20/25-colleges-with-the-best-return-on-investment/.

"CNN Money's How Much Will That College Really Cost?" Cable News Network, 2013, http://cgi.money.cnn.com/tools/collegecost/collegecost.html.

"CNN Money's Colleges with the Highest-Paid Grads," Cable News Network, 2013, http://money.cnn.com/gallery/real_estate/2013/09/12/highest-paid-graduates/index.html.

"College Board Big Future College Search," *The College Board*, 2013, https://bigfuture.collegeboard.org/college-search.

"CollegeCalc College Price Rankings*,"* CollegeCalc.org, 2013, http://www.collegecalc.org/.

"College Confidential College Search," *Hobsons, Inc.*, 2011, http://www.collegeconfidential.com/college_search/.

"COLLEGEdata College Match," *COLLEGEdata*, 2013, http://www.collegedata.com/cs/search/college/college_search_tmpl.jhtml.

"Colleges with the Highest Four-Year Graduation Rates," CollegeXpress, Carnegie Communications, 2013, http://www.collegexpress.com/lists/list/colleges-with-the-highest-four-year-graduation-rates/664/.

"College InSight," The Institute for College Access & Success, 2012, http://college-insight.org.

"College Rankings," *College Prowler*, 2013, http://collegeprowler.com/rankings/.

"COLLEGESTATS.org," *College Stats*, 2013, http://collegestats.org/.

"EduLAUNCHPAD's How to Search Colleges," *eduLAUNCHPAD.com*, 2012, http://www.edulaunchpad.com/Search-Colleges/How-to-Search-Colleges/How-to-Search-Colleges/.

"Fastweb College Search," *Fastweb*, 2013, http://colleges.fastweb.com/.

C. Fairchild, "Student Loan Debt Will Exceed Median Annual Income For College Grads By 2023: Analysis," *The Huffington Post*, July 10, 2013, http://www.huffingtonpost.com/2013/07/10/student-loan-debt-median-income_n_3573683.html.

"Kiplinger Best Values in Public Colleges," *The Kiplinger Washington Editors*, 2013, http://www.kiplinger.com/article/college/T014-C000-S002-best-values-in-public-colleges-2013.html.

R. Morse, "Best Undergraduate Teaching Rankings Methodology," *U.S. News & World Report*, September 9, 2013, http://www.usnews.com/education/best-colleges/articles/2013/09/09/best-undergraduate-teaching-rankings-methodology.

R. Morse, "Rise in Endowments May Impact Best Colleges Rankings," *U.S. News & World Report LP*, February 9, 2012, http://www.usnews.com/education/blogs/college-rankings-blog/2012/02/09/rise-in-endowments-may-impact-best-colleges-rankings.

"NerdScholar," NerdWallet, Inc., 2013, http://www.nerdwallet.com/nerdscholar/grad_surveys/top-salaries.

A. Paulson, "Colleges with the best value? New rankings upend conventional wisdom (+video)," *Christian Science Monitor*, August 27, 2013, http://www.csmonitor.com/USA/Education/2013/0827/Colleges-with-the-best-value-New-rankings-upend-conventional-wisdom-video.

"PayScale College Education ROI Rankings," *PayScale, Inc.*, 2013, http://www.payscale.com/college-education-value-2013.

"Peterson's College Search," *Peterson's, a Nelnet Company*, and its licenses, 2013, http://www.petersons.com/college-search.aspx.

"U.S. Department of Education College Affordability and Transparency Center," U.S. Department of Education, *2013*, http://collegecost.ed.gov/catc/.

"U.S. Department of Education College Navigator," U.S. Department of Education, 2013, http://nces.ed.gov/collegenavigator/.

"U.S. Department of Education College Scorecard," U.S. Department of Education, 2013, http://www.whitehouse.gov/issues/education/

higher-education/college-score-card.

"U.S. Department of Education IPEDS Data Center," U.S. Department of Education, 2013, http://nces.ed.gov/ipeds/.

"U.S. News & World Report's Best Value Schools," *U.S. News & World Report LP.*, 2013, http://colleges.usnews.rankingsandreviews. com/best-colleges/rankings/national-universities/best-value.

"Washington Monthly College Guide," *Washington Monthly, 2013*, http://www.washingtonmonthly.com/college_guide/index.php.

D. C. Weiss, "Law School Grades More Important to Career than Elite School, Researchers Say." *American Bar Association Journal*, 2013, http://www.abajournal.com/news/article/law_school_grades_ more_important_to_paycheck_than_elite_school_researchers.

J. V. Wellman, D.M. Desrochers and C.M. Lenihan, "The Growing Imbalance: Recent Trends in U.S. Postsecondary Education Finance," Delta Project on Postsecondary Education Costs, Productivity and Accountability, 2008, http://www.google.com/url?sa =t&rct=j&q=&esrc=s&source=web&cd=1&ved=0CDEQFjAA&url=ht tp%3A%2F%2Fwww.deltacostproject.org%2Fresources%2Fpdf%2 Fimbalance20080423.pdf&ei=Hv9AUqyuGNKx4APTkYHYAQ&usg =AFQjCNEJAm1wgt7zN5NZFXMP2yjRLHdMnQ&sig2=COlLuqBr2 jyFHJ5kFLAzVg&bvm=bv.52434380,d.dmg.

"What Will They Learn?" American Council of Trustees and Alumni, *What Will They Learn?* 2013, http://www.whatwilltheylearn.com/.

Chapter 16

P. Faris, "Tips for Negotiating Financial Aid for College," ABC News, Apr 29, 2013, http://abcnews.go.com/blogs/headlines/2013/04/tips-for-negotiating-financial-aid-for-college/.

A. Kari, "Duquesne to Cut Tuition, Fees in Half for New Education Majors," TribLive News, August 7, 2011, http://triblive.com/x/

pittsburghtrib/news/breaking/s_752007.html#axzz2Vp87B5sb.

K. Knight, "15 Weird Scholarships," *Fastweb*, 2013, http://www.fastweb.com/college-scholarships/articles/2859-15-weird-scholarships?page=3.

R. Perez-Pena, "College Offers Top Applicants Two-Thirds Off," *New York Times*," September 28, 2011, http://www.nytimes.com/2011/09/29/nyregion/seton-hall-university-to-offer-steep-tuition-discounts.html.

M. Schifrin, "Tuition Discount Alert: 50 Great Colleges Desperately Seeking Students," May 14, 2013, *Forbes.com LLC*, http://www.forbes.com/sites/schifrin/2013/05/14/tuition-discount-alert-50-great-colleges-desperately-seeking-students/.

Postscript

G.D. Di Lampedusa, *The Leopard: A Novel* (New York: *Pantheon*, 2007).

Chart Data Sources

Administrative Costs Increased Faster than Any Other College Expenses, 1993–2007

J. P. Green, "Administrative Bloat at American Universities: The Real Reason for High Costs in Higher Education," The Goldwater Institute, 2010, http://goldwaterinstitute.org/sites/default/files/Administrative%20Bloat.pdf.

Average Freshmen Tuition Discount Rates

N. P. Davis, "Demand Drives Discount Rates," National Association of College and University Business Officers, June, 2013, http://www.nacubo.org/Business_Officer_Magazine/Magazine_Archives/June_2013/Demand_Drives_Discount_Rates.html.

L. L. Hubbell and L. Lapovsky, "Tuition Discounting: 15 Years in Perspective," National Association of College and University Business Officers, 2004, http://www.nacubo.org/Business_Officer_Magazine/Business_Officer_Plus/Online_Articles/Tuition_Discounting_15_Years_in_Perspective.html.

N. Pullaro, "2011 Survey of Tuition Discounting Study Report," National Association of College and University Business Officers, 2012, http://www.nacubo.org/Research/Research_News/2011_NACUBO_Tuition_Discounting_Study_Released.html.

Average Percentage of College Budgets Spent on Instruction and Student Services

J. E. Morley Jr., "Explaining College Costs," National Association of College and University Business Officers, February, 2002, http://www.nacubo.org/Research/NACUBO_Research_Projects/College_Pricing_and_Financial_Aid/Cost_of_College_Study.html.

Average Student Loan Debt (in 2011 Dollars)

R. Fry, "A Record One-in-Five Households Now Owe Student Loan Debt," Pew Research Social & Demographic Trends, Pew Research Center, September 26, 2012, http://www.pewsocialtrends.org/2012/09/26/a-record-one-in-five-households-now-owe-student-loan-debt/.

College Graduates Starting Salaries Have Fallen

H. Shierholz, "New College Grads Losing Ground on Wages," Economic Policy Institute, August 31, 2011, http://www.epi.org/publication/new_college_grads_losing_ground_on_wages/.

Median Student Debt for a Graduate Degree (in 2012 Dollars)

J. Delisle, "The Graduate Student Debt Review," New America Education Policy Program, March, 2014, http://newamerica.net/sites/newamerica.net/files/policydocs/GradStudentDebtReview-Delisle-Final.pdf.

Percent Change in College Tuition vs. Other Costs Since 1978

Consumer Price Index, Division of Consumer Prices and Price Indexes, U.S. Bureau of Labor Statistics, January 16, 2013, http://www.bls.gov.

Percentage of Full-Time Faculty Teaching 9 or More Hours Per Week

S. Hurtado, K. Eagan, J.H. Pryor, H. Whang, and S. Tran, "Undergraduate Teaching Faculty: The 2010–11 HERI Faculty Survey," Higher Education Research Institute, University of California, Los Angeles, 2012, http://www.heri.ucla.edu/monographs/HERI-FAC2011-Monograph.pdf.

Projected Change in High School Graduates by Region, 2011–2028

"Knocking at the Door, Projections of High school Graduates," Western Interstate Commission for Higher Education, December 2012, http://www.wiche.edu/pub/16556.

Projected 30-Year Change in Composition of U.S. High School Graduates by Race/Ethnicity

"Knocking at the Door, Projections of High School Graduates," Western Interstate Commission for Higher Education, December 2012, http://www.wiche.edu/pub/16556.

Student Loan Debt vs. Credit Card Debt

Quarterly Report on Household Debt and Credit, 2012, Q3," Federal Reserve Bank of New York, 2013, http://www.newyorkfed.org/householdcredit/.

Total College Construction Costs

P. Abramson, "Slow and Steady," 19th Annual College Construction Report, *College Planning & Management,* February, 2014, http://webcpm.com/research/2014/02/college-construction-report/asset.aspx?tc=assetpg.

About the Authors

Robert V. Iosue

EDUCATION

Adelphi University, Garden City, New York – 1971
Doctor of Philosophy.

Thesis: "Research in the Field of Non-Linear Wave Motion."

Adelphi University, Garden City, New York – 1963
Master of Science.

Columbia University, New York City – 1958
Master of Arts.

Fitchburg State College - 1955
Bachelor of Science

SCHOLARSHIP

"Calculus of Variation" **by Marvin Forray – 1968**
Contributed the last chapter.

"Pythagoras Fortran and the Classical method", **by Robert V. Iosue – 1972**
New York State Mathematics Teachers Journal

MILITARY

Ist Lieutenant, First Marine Air Wing – 1955-57

United States Marine Corps, honorable discharge.

PROFESSIONAL EXPERIENCE

President and Professor of Mathematics, York College of Pennsylvania – 1976-91

Some of the accomplishments made over the 15 years that were touted in the media were: SAT scores improved by 200 points, faculty salaries moved from the fifth quintile to the first quintile for all colleges, and most important of all, this was accomplished while keeping tuition increases BELOW the CPI for the entire 15 years.

Assistant Dean, Dean, Vice President of Academic Affairs, CW Post of Long Island University – 1970-76

Responsible for faculty and academic programs; continued teaching math.

Instructor, Assistant Professor, Associate Professor of Mathematics, CW Post of Long Island University 1960-70

Taught all levels of math from freshmen to graduate.

Graduate Teaching Assistant, School of Engineering and School of Architecture, Columbia University, New York, NY – 1959-60

GED Program for Marines without a High School Diploma – 1957

OTHER TEACHING EXPERIENCE

Scholar in Residence, Suburban High School – 1973-74

Prepared gifted students for County Math Fair.

Higher Education Opportunity Program – 1971-72

Taught math courses for economically disadvantaged students.

Descriptive Geometry, Farmingdale State College – 1965

Continued teaching math while leading the College.

GRANTS

Higher Education Opportunity Grant – 1971-72

Developed remedial math program at CW Post for disadvantaged students who did not graduate from high school.

HONORS

Honorary Doctorate of Humane Letters, York College of Pennsylvania

Honorary Alumnus, York College of Pennsylvania

Alumni Medal, Adelphi University

Featured in U.S. Information Agency Video

Produced for South Africa; topic was funding

CONSULTING

**Lancaster Theological Seminary, Lancaster, Pennsylvania
1996**

Financial concerns.

Hebron Academy, Hebron, Maine – 1993-95

Leadership problems and financial concerns.

Southern Seminary College, Roanoke, Virginia – 1992

Financial concerns.

Cleveland School System, Cleveland, Ohio – 1983

Provided a review of changes needed in college preparatory programs. At the time, the entire school system was under city control for financial mismanagement, and under court control for affirmative action concerns.

State University System of New York – 1970-71

Developed Cooperative College Center Math Curriculum.

SPECIAL COMMITTEES

Governor Thornburgh of Pennsylvania appointee to a Blue Ribbon Commission, PA Bar Association – 1997-98

Consider changing the system of Superior and Supreme Court judges from elected to selected.

President Reagan appointee to a Congressional Advisory Committee on Student Financial Aid – 1987-90

Charged with improving the system then used.

CONGRESSIONAL TESTIMONY ON HIGHER EDUCATION COSTS

Select Committee on Education and Labor, House of Representatives – 1992

The title: "College Education: Paying more and Getting Less." Although the committee was sympathetic, only in Colorado were some changes made as a result of Representative Patricia Schroeder's help.

Committee on Education and Labor, House of Representatives – 1987

A continuation of the 1985 Committee hearings on ineffective use of funds.

Committee on Education and Labor, House of Representatives – 1985

The first of three hearings in which testimony was provided about where money was being wasted and how the government was misdirected by college lobbyists.

PUBLISHED BOOKS

"Fun and games on Campus: And how College Presidents Earn Their Big Dollars" by Robert V. Iosue 2012

Published by Amazon. A light and humorous look at a variety of incidents that occur at every college in the country, and how presidents react.

"Starting College" by Robert V. Iosue – 1992-3

Published by Wellspring Publishers in 1992, revised in 1993. A briefer for college-bound students. Approximately 20,000 sold.

BOOK REVIEWS

"Altering Collective Bargaining" – 1977

Published by Journal of Law and Education.

"Law and the Student Press" – 1975

Published by Journal of Law and Education.

SELECTED ARTICLES, 1973-2013

"Who Pays For the High Cost of Low Tuition?"
Newsday

"A Day in the Life of a College President"
AGB Reports

"There are Things Colleges Can Do When Aid is Cut"
The Chronicle of Higher Education

"Cutting Aid is Not a Bad Idea"
The Baltimore Sun

"Do Europeans Share Our Education concerns?"
AGB Reports

"Limited Options Under Unlimited Retirement Age"
Higher Education and National Affairs

"How Colleges Can Cut Costs"
The Wall Street Journal

"College: The High Cost of declining Productivity"
Academic Questions

"Controlling Costs for a Lean Administration"
Journal, National Association of College Auxiliary Services

"Insights on Higher Education"
Forum for Applied Research and Public Policy

"Gilding the Steeples"
The Washington Times

"Crossing Cultures"
American Association for Higher Education

FEATURED IN:

The Chronicle of Higher Education, The Wall Street Journal, Newsday, The Washington Times, Forbes, Insight, The San Diego Union, The Education Record, School and College, The Philadelphia Inquirer.

CITED IN:

U.S. News and World Report, The Philadelphia Inquirer, Readers Digest, Chicago tribune, The Chronicle of Higher Education, The New York Times, The Wall Street Journal, The Washington Times, Newsday, The Baltimore Sun, Newsweek, Barron's best Buys in Higher Education.

OTHER MEDIA, 1976-2013:

Various national and local television and radio program interviews; book club presentations; book signings.

Frank Mussano

EDUCATION

Nova Southeastern University, Fort Lauderdale, Florida 4/76-10/78

Ed.D. College Administration

Dissertation: "The development of Procedures for Assisting Resident Students in Selecting Housing Facilities Which Provide the Most Compatible Social Climate."

University of Maryland, College Park, Maryland 2/71-6/72

M.Ed. Counseling and Personnel Services

The Pennsylvania State University, University Park, Pennsylvania – 9/66-12/70

B.S. Secondary Education – English

PROFESSIONAL EXPERIENCE

Dean of Administrative Services, York College of Pennsylvania – 7/87-7/13

Developed and coordinated creative enrollment management strategies encompassing research, publicity, market segmentation, recruitment and retention programs; supervised Information Technology, Admissions, Financial Aid, Continuing Studies, Academic Advising, Records and Registrar's Offices. Implemented the campus computer network. Served on various campus-wide committees, including Long Range Planning Committee, Middle States Accreditation Review Committee, Information Technology Task Force, and the Council on Religious Activities.

Dean of Student Affairs, York College of Pennsylvania 10/81-6/87

Coordinated all student service departments including Residence Life, Student Activities, Counseling and Testing, Career Services, Intercollegiate Athletics and Health Services; supervised divisional research and publications, freshmen orientation programming, registration processing and standards for student conduct.

Director of Student Activities and the Student Union, York College of Pennsylvania – 3/77-10/81

Coordinated all non-academic student programming including freshmen orientation, lectures, concerts, film series, special events, etc. Directed the intramural department, gymnasium, fitness center and swimming pool personnel. Formally advised the Student Government, Interfraternal Panhellenic Council and other organizations. Coordinated all operations within the Student Union. Established the Student Orientation Program.

Director of Residence Life and Counselor, York College of Pennsylvania – 2/74-6/77

Trained and supervised resident directors, student advisors, custodians, and maintenance personnel in residence halls, apartment complex and mini-houses. Directed Peer Advising Program, Judicial Board, Food Services Committee, Residence Council, etc. Coordinated student disciplinary sanctions.

COMMUNITY

Life Member, York Agricultural Society, York, PA 1/12-Present

President, National Kidney Foundation of York County 7/96-7/98

Founding Board Member, St. Paul's Lutheran Church

Day Care Center, York, PA – 9/94-7/96

Fundraising Chair, National Kidney Foundation of York County, York, PA – 9/76 - 7/96

Research Coordinator, Rehabilitation and Industrial Training Center, York, PA – 6/72 - 6/74

PROFESSIONAL AWARDS

York College Professional Service and Leadership Award – 5/01

Presented for displaying the highest qualities of leadership and Distinction

Student Senate Administrator Recognition Award – 4/98

Honoring the administrator who contributes most to the student body.

PUBLICATIONS AND PRESENTATIONS

"Higher Education Landscape" and "Freshmen Profile" 5/06-5/13

Enrollment environment updates formally presented annually to Board of Trustees, Alumni Association, Long Range Planning Committee and Academic Senate

"Key Indicators 1990-2012", in:

"Building a Better College – York College of Pennsylvania Transforms through Strategic Planning"

by George W. Waldner, published by York College of Pennsylvania. Created nineteen key indicator data charts.

"Marketing Your Price" – 11/11

Presented at the American Marketing Association Conference in Chicago, Illinois.

"The Impact of Demographic Changes on Higher Education" – 7/05

College Board Forum Panel Discussion, Philadelphia, Pa.

"How a Small Private College Beat the Demographic Doldrums" – 1/94

Guest Editorial, Admissions Marketing Report

"AS/400 Boosts Productivity at York College" – 3/92

The Higher Education Journal

"Beating the Demographic Slump" – 3/92

Recruitment and Retention in Higher Education

"Personal Education at a Low Cost" – 1/89

Admissions Marketing Report

"A Model Summer Freshmen Explorientation Program" – 1982

The Education Resource Information Center Clearinghouse

"The Effects of a Study Skills Workshop Upon Study Techniques, Study Organization and Study Motivation for Volunteer Resident Freshmen" – 3/78

Resources in Education

"Personal Management Style as it Relates to Effective Governance in York College Residence Facilities" – 6/77

Resources in Education

"A Student Operated Resource Center" – 12/76

National Association of student Personnel Administrators Journal

"York College Student Resource Center" – 4/76

Presented at the Annual Conference of the Pennsylvania Association of Colleges